The Great Adventure—Untold

Charles Hamman

Burning Daylight

Published by Burning Daylight an imprint of
Pearn and Associates, Inc.
1600 Edora Court Suite D
Fort Collins, Colorado 80525
For information about publishing please
contact happypoet@hotmail.com.

Cover design by Anne Kilgore
Special thanks to Meme' for editing this so we can read it.

Library of Congress Control Number: 2011933632

Hamman, Charles 1949
The Great Adventure Untold, by Charles Hamman.
First edition.

ISBN 978-0-9841683-8-5 cloth

PRINTED IN THE UNITED STATES OF AMERICA
Canada, United Kingdom, Europe, and Australia

First edition

Dedicated to

My grandchildren and
their Great Grandfather J.P. Hamman, for without
his guidance this adventure could not be told.

Keep your powder dry

Always aim high—but true

Walk softly and

Remember always—Semper Fi

Contents

INTRODUCTION

The first time I saw Mt. Rushmore I was captivated by its majesty. The huge white granite sculptures stood in sharp contrast against the blue sky and the black hills. Here, in this hallowed place, on the sacred ground of the Sioux Indian resides a monument immortalizing four American presidents: George Washington, Abraham Lincoln, Thomas Jefferson, and Theodore Roosevelt. Immediately my mind conjured up images of paintings that I had seen at the Smithsonian Institute and Natural History Museum. I recalled paintings of George Washington ("the Father of our nation") the first President consoling the troops at Valley Forge, or standing up in a boat crossing the Delaware River pointing the way to battle. And Abraham Lincoln ("the Savior of our Nation") the sixteenth President, standing tall at the podium with his tall black hat delivering his famous speech, "A house divided against itself cannot stand," and another painting of him delivering The Gettysburg Address. Of Thomas Jefferson, our third President, I recalled a painting of him, sitting down, quill pen in hand, surrounded by Ben Franklin, John Adams, and others that had "pledged their lives, their fortunes, their sacred honor." These were the Founding Fathers, and they entrusted Thomas Jefferson with the monumental task of writing the Declaration of Independence, for

Thomas Jefferson was the pen of the American Revolution as George Washington was the sword. I did not know it at the time, but Thomas Jefferson and John Adams, our 2nd President, both died on the same day, July 4, 1826—the 50th anniversary of the Declaration of Independence.

Finally, there at the very back was Theodore Roosevelt, our 26th President. I paused and wondered, how did he get up there? Surely it wasn't because he led the Rough Riders on a charge up San Juan Hill.

There had to be more to it than that. The one thing I was sure of, they all had something in common—CHARACTER!

In time, I would come to learn that it was precisely that "character," indeed "enormous character" that put Theodore Roosevelt (TR) in the company of these great men.

THE CHALLENGE

One might ask, "How do you get enough character to get your face carved onto the side of a mountain?" The key word is "get." Because character is gotten or acquired over time by learning through experience, and it is developed in us when we make choices between right and wrong.

In contrast, morals can be taught by our parents, our church, our schools, and even our friends. What is legally correct or incorrect can also be taught through a study of the law.

But character, on the other hand, must be developed. The dictionary defines character as "a distinctive trait, quality, or attribute; the pattern of behavior or personality found in an individual or group; the moral constitution, self-discipline, fortitude, good reputation."

Moral is defined as "relating to, dealing with or capable of making the distinction between right and wrong in conduct; good or right in conduct or character; based on the principles of right conduct rather than legality." Also sprinkled about in the definition are the words ethical, virtuous, integrity, righteous.

Perhaps the simplest definition of character was best stated by Congressman J.C. Watts of Oklahoma when he quoted his father, "Character means doing what's right when nobody's looking."

Theodore Roosevelt said this,

"Character is far more important than intellect in making a man a good citizen or successful at his calling—meaning by character not only such qualities as honesty and truthfulness, but courage, perseverance and self-reliance."

All of these words give rise to the meaning of character. And it is developed when we make choices between right and wrong.

CHOICES

On March 15, 1783, George Washington was approached by officers of the Continental Army, of which he was the Commander In Chief. They stated that they wanted to make him King of the United States, by armed intervention if necessary. He refused, stating that this should not become a country of monarchs or kings. They would not listen, and continued to voice their anger and displeasure with their new country. He urged them to reconsider their actions and not fan the flames of dissention. Then he produced a letter that he had received from a Congressman stating that this new democracy would address their concerns and treat them fairly. As he began reading the letter he stopped and appeared puzzled. The men became concerned and began to sense that something was wrong. The room grew quiet. In a dramatic moment, Washington pulled out a pair of eyeglasses which no one had ever seen him do before. As he put them on, he said, *"Gentlemen, you will permit me to put on my spectacles, for I have not only grown gray but almost blind in the service of my country."* Those simple words would alter the course of history. The men had never before seen General Washington so humble, and saw clearly his deep commitment to our nation and to liberty. They realized how wrong they were in thinking only of themselves and not the future of their country.

The choice he made was not as simple as it might seem. How many men would have turned down the opportunity to become King of the United States? Washington did! However, he did agree to accept a nomination by which the electors would vote him in as President for eight years, but only eight years. The choice was his. For him it was a choice between right and wrong. A matter of principle, that the country's best interests should be placed ahead of his own personal gain. His integrity would become the cornerstone of his character.

Not always in life are choices made clear. In fact sometimes we are given no choice at all. Theodore Roosevelt borrowed a quote from Leslie Buswell to describe what actually is dealing with destiny rather than making choices, *"We are free to face our destiny and we must meet it with a high and resolute courage."* Military annals are replete with examples of men meeting destiny with resolute courage. These are the times when we must draw upon our reservoirs of character.

When you tour the battlefield at the Little Big Horn, it does not take a person long to figure out what happened. Artist renderings and some history books would have us believe that Custer, surrounded by his men, chose to make a desperate stand on the open prairie, against overwhelming force, where upon they all died. Parts of that are true. But in reality, there were no choices to be made and little opportunity to decide right from wrong and little chance to build upon character. It was time to draw from the reservoirs of existing character, and it had better be full. Destiny meeting resolute courage. The men in Custer's command did not have any choice on where they would be on June 25, 1876. Custer had his orders, and he was given broad discretion in executing them. He came to the Little Big Horn to engage and destroy the Indians that were camped on the river. Upon arriving at the Little Big Horn he split his forces into three groups. Custer led 212 men along a ridge overlooking the river. In his company were his brother Captain Tom Custer, another younger brother 19 year old Boston Custer, a 16 year old nephew Autie Reed, and a brother-in-law Lieutenant Calhoun. Before they could make it to the river, Custer and all 212 men in his immediate command were killed. It took less than an hour and a half.

White marble grave markers are used to show where the men died. They are scattered over a wide area along the ridge, and, for the most part, they tell the story. You can actually drive a car through the battle area. Custer's men were not able to form a defensive perimeter. They were not given a choice to make with regard to surrender. Nor could they escape. They died wherever they were trapped. Only 42 men actually died in the immediate vicinity of Custer. The Indians did not charge into Custer's gunfire mounted on horseback as many historical depictions show. They did not have to. They surrounded the battle area, encircled pockets of dispersed troops and rained arrows and lead down on them until they succumbed to the intense barrage. Consequently, only two Indian ponies were found dead at the scene. In contrast, 70 cavalry horses were found dead, 42 on Custer hill—most of those killed by the troops so that they could use the dead horses as cover. There was so much lead in the air that Custer's men could not even put up an effective fight. Indian accounts of the battle say that many troopers did make one choice, suicide. The Indians did not have to mount a massive frontal assault, which explains why best estimates put Indian losses at less than 30 dead. Besides a small monument with the names of the soldiers, there is only the desolate prairie of buffalo grass and lonely white marble grave markers.

The Battle of the Little Big Horn was a national disaster. Custer's 7th Cavalry went into the Little Big Horn with 625 men. 265 died. The most studied consensus puts total Indian losses for all skirmishes at 40. A Court of Inquiry was convened to find out what happened. Did Custer disobey his orders? From that Inquiry one recurring question seems to surface. And that is the question of his character. The fact that his character was constantly in question throughout the Inquiry is most interesting. Custer was a West Point graduate, a highly decorated Civil War hero, had 11 horses shot out from under him, made Brigadier General at 23—the youngest General in U.S. military history. He was there when Lee surrendered to Grant. He had been in numerous Indian battles and won them all. There was no doubt about his courage. That is why he was sent to the Little Big Horn. His courage and fighting abilities were widely known and respected among the Indians. In fact, because of their respect, his was the only body found at the Little Big Horn not horribly mutilated. They never even lifted his yellow hair. In contrast, his brother's body Capt. Tom Custer was so horribly mutilated that it was unrecognizable except for a tattoo, TWC. Apparently, the Indians were not informed that Tom Custer was a two-time Medal of Honor winner. Despite all of Custer's heroic deeds, the Court of Inquiry then and historians to this day still debate his character. Prior to the Court of Inquiry he had already been court-martialed once and threatened again with still another court-martial. The character questions revolve around the issue of did he risk the lives of his men for personal glory? Did he disobey his orders? Why didn't he wait for reinforcements before attacking the Indians? Did he want all of the glory for himself? Why did he have a newspaper correspondent along and his kid brother Boston and young Autie? To the question of disobeying orders, the answer is no, he did not. To other questions, we can only speculate. But still the questions of his character persist. Ironically, the Indian chief who led the final assault against Custer was Chief Crazy Horse. But, there has never been a question regarding his character. His image is being carved on the side of a mountain not too far from Mt. Rushmore.

If words could provide solace to honor all of those on both sides, perhaps this quote from TR would be appropriate.

"There are good men and bad men of all nationalities, creeds, and colors; and if this world of ours is ever to become what we hope someday it may become, it must be by the general recognition that the man's heart and soul, the man's worth and actions, determine his standing."

When we are allowed decisions between right and wrong, the result can have profound consequences in building character not only in ourselves and others around us, but also in our schools, our work, even our country.

TR wrote,

"I honor beyond measure those who do their full duty . . . and all the more because the doing of duty generally means pain, hardship, self-mastery, self-denial, endurance of risk, of labor, of irksome monotony, wearing effort, steady perseverance under difficulties and discouragement."

The profound consequences of building character in a nation through building character in men is easily understood when you step through the doors of the Alamo. Many people think that the story of the Alamo is similar to that of the Little Big Horn, men meeting ill-fate through military blunder, but that is not the case. The defenders of the Alamo made a lot of choices between right and wrong. Each time, they would build character in themselves, the people of the Republic of Texas, and ultimately our nation.

When you first walk through the doors of the Alamo, there is a placard listing the names of the defenders and where they were from. I was surprised to notice how many were from foreign countries. The vast majority were from the southern states, with about two dozen from Tennessee and two dozen actually from Texas. Then it dawned on me; they were all foreigners. The Alamo belonged to Mexico. These guys took it, and then died defending it. The one thing they all had in common was that they did it by their own choice. They firmly believed that it was the right thing to do.

Initially, the Mexican government invited people to come and settle in their Province of Texas. People came from all around. Then the Mexican government levied taxes and laws that were unacceptable to the inhabitants, so they rebelled with the idea to make the Mexican Province of Texas an independent country—The Republic of Texas. At this point the inhabitants of Texas made their first choice—to fight for their independence and a better way of life for their families. Letters were sent out around the country. *"Let each man come with a good rifle and 100 rounds of ammunition—and come soon."* And they did. By their own choice because they believed it was right.

On January 19, 1836, the "fightingest man in Texas" Colonel Jim Bowie rode into the Alamo with 30-some men. There was already a force of approximately 70 men occupying the Alamo. Sam Houston, the commander of the "Army of Texas," had given orders to Bowie to consolidate the forces, blow up the Alamo, and pull back. But he also gave Bowie wide discretion. Bowie decided to stay, with full knowledge that General Santa Ana was on his way. On February 3, Colonel William Travis showed up with 30 men. On February 8, Congressman-Colonel David Crockett arrived with more than a dozen Tennessee mounted volunteers. He addressed the Texans:

"I have come to your country, though not, I hope, through any selfish motive whatever. I have come to aid you all that I can in your noble cause. I shall identify myself with your interests, and all the honor that I desire is that of defending, as a high private, in common with my fellow citizens, the liberties of our common country."

Men were making choices—and they were deadly serious. On February 23, the Mexican army began to appear. The two sides sent emissaries to meet. The Mexicans demanded surrender and they would spare the lives of the Texans. Travis decided to answer with a shattering blast from an 18-pound cannon. On February 24, Travis assumed command from Bowie, as Bowie was stricken with typhoid pneumonia. The siege was on. Travis sent the following message to the people of Texas and the nation:

"Fellow citizens and compatriots, I am besieged by a thousand or more Mexicans under Santa Ana . . . . I shall never surrender or retreat. Then, I call on you in the name of liberty of patriotism, and everything dear to the American character, to come to our aid . . . Victory or Death."

At this point in time, it was obvious to all inside the Alamo and outside that death was certain in the face of overwhelming forces. On March 1, 32 men led by George Kimball, a hat maker from New York, broke through the Mexican lines and entered the Alamo. On March 3, Jim Bonham, a lawyer from South Carolina and an excellent horseman, broke through the Mexican ranks into the Alamo. The defenders now numbered 183. Santa Ana had an army of 2,500.

It is most interesting, as the chronology of events unfold, that men are choosing to break into the Alamo—not out of the Alamo! On March 5, Travis assembled the men. He explained that there was no longer any hope of help. Their only choice was to surrender, escape, or fight. And every man would make his own choice. He went on to say that if any man wanted to escape, to "step out of ranks." He then withdrew his saber and scratched a line in the dirt. Those that were going to join him had to step across the line. Jim Bowie with his famous oversized Arkansas "toothpick" of a knife asked to be carried across. He would be followed by the Texans, then Davy Crockett and the volunteers. One man chose to step out of ranks. His name was Louis Rose. On March 6, the final assault began. It was over in less than two hours. Their bodies were stacked, soaked in oil, and burned, all 182. The Alamo is their tombstone; the great state of Texas is their memorial.

They made a lot of choices and built a lot of character before deciding to die for their values. They firmly believed that their sacrifice would enflame Texans and the American people to rally to their cause, thereby making Texas a state and a place where their families could enjoy "life, liberty, and the pursuit of happiness." Their character became immortalized in history. The nation was grateful and manifest destiny was born. "Thermopylae had its messengers of death, but the Alamo had none."

TR wrote:

"In the long fight for righteousness the watchword for all of us is spend and be spent. It is little matter whether any one man fails or succeeds; but the cause should not fail, for it is the cause of mankind."

BAD MEN

As we travel through life we also encounter bad character. We know it when we see it. Virtually every night on the evening news we are subjected to more bad character than good character. Bad character is easier to develop than good character. Simply defy the principles of decency, moral conduct, ethical behavior, lie, dishonor oneself, cheat, break the law, make choices between right and wrong that are not rooted in righteousness and impugn one's integrity and you might make the evening news. Theodore Roosevelt said this,

> *"Measure iniquity by the heart, whether a man's purse be full or empty, partly full or partly empty. If the man is a decent man, whether well off or not well off, stand by him; if he is not a decent man stand against him, whether he be rich or poor."*

In Wyoming, near the Big Horn Mountains is a place called the "Hole in the Wall." This was the hideout of many notorious outlaws of the late 1800's. I had the opportunity to ride into the Hole in the Wall with the Larimer County Sheriff's Posse and retrace the path of these notorious outlaws. Such men as the James Brothers, Butch Cassidy's "Hole in the Wall Gang," and Cole Younger's gang. The canyon was more than ten miles long, steep on both sides, and impossible for lawmen to travel without being ambushed.

The villains robbed pillaged, plundered, raped, and murdered collectively hundreds of our citizens. But in the assessment of bad character and to whom we might pin the award for "worst character in American history," they look like church mice who had lost their way. In pursuit of placing the award, I thought about all of the notorious serial killers I had seen on TV: crazed maniac killers such as Charles Manson; smooth, charismatic, deadly killers like Ted Bundy and Son of Sam; even butchers such as Jeffrey Dahmer. I couldn't leave out Timothy McViegh from the contest. He blew up the Federal Building in Oklahoma City and killed 168 of our fellow citizens. But all of these nominees pale in comparison. Through the ashes of a great Civil War, fought to establish right from wrong, grew the nation's award winner, Captain Henry Wirz—the "Butcher of Andersonville."

Henry Wirz has the distinction of being the only person to be put on trial by the Federal Government and executed for war crimes. He was the commandant of the Confederate prison at Andersonville, Georgia. More than 13,000 Union soldiers died at Andersonville. They died mostly from typhoid, pneumonia, smallpox, diarrhea, dysentery, maltreatment, and murder. At one point, prisoners died at the rate of 150 per day. The prison was nothing more than a concentration camp, the likes of which our country had never seen before Hitler's death camps after WW II. The country was horrified, and Henry Wirz became the most hated man in America. He claimed during the trial that he was only following orders. Whose orders? He was offered a pardon if he would testify that former Confederate

President Jefferson Davis was responsible for the deaths at Andersonville. Wirz refused and stated that it wasn't true. Indeed it wasn't. Jefferson Davis had actually written letters to the Lincoln administration requesting a reinstatement of the prisoner exchange program, which the Union had stopped. The Union refused. He also cited the fact that the South did not have the necessary provisions and medical supplies to properly care for the prisoners. Jefferson Davis made a humane effort to purchase medical supplies with gold. But the North had imposed an embargo on such goods. His requests fell on deaf ears.

Wirz wrote two profoundly eloquent letters pleading for mercy and pardon for himself—one to President Johnson and one to his attorney. But where were the letters pleading relief for the 13,000 men that he buried? Eloquent letters, pages wet with tears, pleading purpose of moral integrity—there weren't any. And there was never any question regarding Henry Wirz's character.

But Henry Wirz was not alone in committing atrocities against Americans. There were others. The North was just as guilty as the South. The most brutal prison belonged to the North, the "Fort Delaware Death Pen" situated on Pea Patch Island in the Delaware Bay. More than 2400 rebs died there—some from torture. At Elmira Prison in New York, a third of the prison population died. The chief surgeon E.L. Sanger boasted that he killed more rebs than any other soldier at the front. The remaining 66 percent were fortunate to subsist on an abundant supply of rats.

As we have had bad character in men, so too we have seen bad character in our nation. Consider these numbers—620,000 Americans died during the Civil War. That is more than have died in all our wars combined throughout our history. Fifty six thousand Americans died during captivity as prisoners during the Civil War. Thousands more would die following their release from prison, not able to recover from their wounds. That is as many as we have names carved on the black wall at the Vietnam War Memorial. If our national character is forever marred from our treatment of Native Americans and the injustice of slavery, then it must also carry an ugly scar from our treatment of each other. Americans had finally had enough of killing Americans, but—Captain Henry Wirz would swing from the gallows.

Perhaps the award for "worst character in America" would be better placed if it were awarded instead to "We the people," for the character of a country can never be stronger than the character of its people.

TR wrote:

"It is character that counts in a nation as in a man."

SUPREME CHARACTER

While it is easy to find examples of bad character and harder to build good character, it is even more difficult to understand "supreme character." Supreme character as I'd define it is that character which comes from deep within the reservoir of one's soul and rises through supreme sacrifice. This is character that cannot be taught, learned, nor developed.

Lance Corporal Roy Wheat, Private First Class (PFC) Danny Skiwoski, Lieutenant James Webb, and me Corporal Hamman, had a couple of things in common besides being Marines. We all fought over the same ground and were all decorated. But only one of us would demonstrate "supreme character" by "supreme sacrifice."

In the Que Son Valley south of DaNang, Vietnam, there was a combat base named An Hoa (pronounced An Wa). Not far from there was a Marine outpost called "Liberty Bridge." It was in this area of the Que Son Valley that we all became acquainted with the term "supreme character." Lt. Webb would become one of the most decorated Marines in Vietnam; two purple Hearts, a Navy Cross, a Silver Star, two Bronze Stars. He was a Platoon and Company Commander, who later became Secretary of the Navy. He also wrote a book *Fields of Fire* that received national acclaim about the ground we fought over in the Que Son Valley. PFC Skiwoski was awarded the Silver Star, and thereby added another chapter in the Marine Corps Fighting Manual amending the section that deals within the section that deals with "how to save yourself and your fellow Marines after you step on a land mine." Corporal "Ham" received the Navy Commendation Medal for Valor in combat and learned about "Semper Fidelis" and another meaning for "walk softly."

PFC Skiwoski, 18 years old, was a point man in my company. One day while leading point for a reinforced squad of Marines on a search and destroy mission, he stepped on a booby trap. The booby trap was a 60 mm mortar round and was activated by a pressure release device. When he stepped down, the pressure release device popped up against the bottom of his boot. The booby trap was now armed but would not activate until your foot was lifted. "Ski" felt the device hit the bottom of his boot. Being alert— he froze. Then he informed the squad leader that he was standing on a land mine with no idea of how big the explosive device was. Together they decided to stack everybody's helmets and flak jackets around Ski's leg. Next they called in a low priority Medivac helicopter. That took 45 minutes. Then the Marines formed a perimeter for a landing zone. The corpsman got his bandages laid out. The chopper was circling overhead. Now it was up to Ski to jump. Fortunately he was standing on a rice paddy dike so that when he jumped, he would drop two to three feet into the mud and below the explosion line. He jumped. The mortar round exploded and Ski received only a minor shrapnel wound. Because of his resourceful actions, his life was sparred and so was that of the deuce point, or the Marine behind him, and probably others in the column. That kind of resourceful and alert attention is taught in training and is updated in the Marine Corps Fighting Manual.

Lance Corporal Roy Wheat was the one that introduced us all to the term "supreme character." He earned the Medal of Honor (MOH). However, the Marine Corps Fighting Manual was not amended to teach what LC Roy Wheat did, because it was not something you could teach. Lance Corporal Roy Wheat, 19 years old, from Moselle, Mississippi, volunteered to lead two guys outside of the defensive perimeter and set up an observation post to watch for enemy movement. While returning, Lance Corporal Wheat tripped a wire attached to a booby trap. He heard the detonator release. Without hesitation, he shouted a warning then hurled himself on the booby trap, absorbing the tremendous explosion with his own body.[1] In that very instant, he decided to trade his life for that of his fellow Marines behind him. He did so knowing full well what the outcome would be. His action went way beyond the call of duty. It was supreme character making supreme sacrifice.

Our nation recognizes and honors conspicuous gallantry by awarding the Medal of Honor, typically given to only the "bravest of the brave." Those that knowingly and willingly trade their lives for others go way beyond the requirements for the MOH. In Vietnam there were 238 MOH's awarded, most posthumously (men who died while performing heroic deeds). Twenty-four men did virtually the same thing as Lance Corporal Wheat—jumping on an explosive device after tripping it, sacrificing themselves for the men around them.

Edward Murphy relates the following story in his book titled *Vietnam Medal of Honor Heroes:*

"Mr. Olive, a father of soldier Milton Lee Olive, from Chicago, Illinois, sent the following letter to President Johnson after his 18-year-old son received his MOH for the very same deed that Lance Corporal Wheat performed. In it he said,

'It is our dream and prayer that someday the Asiatics, the Europeans, the Israelites, the Africans, the Australians, the Latins, and the Americans can all live in One-World. It is our hope that in our country the Klansmen, the Negroes, the Hebrews, and the Catholics will sit down together in the common purpose of goodwill and dedication; that the moral and creative intelligence of our united people will pick up the chalice of wisdom and place it upon the mountaintop of human integrity; that all mankind, from all the earth, shall resolve 'to study war no more.'"

The City of Chicago honored its deceased warrior hero by naming in his memory a junior college, a lakefront park, and a portion of the McCormick Place convention center, memorializing the essence of "supreme character" meeting "supreme sacrifice."

CREED AND CULTURE

All Marines carry with them the motto, "Semper Fidelis," in short, Semper Fi. It means, "Always faithful." In these two words is their creed. In essence, it defines the character of the United States Marine Corps. It is a character that the entire world has come to respect and admire. There is probably no more easily recognized symbol of our country anywhere in the world—aside from the Stars and Stripes itself, than a Marine in dress uniform. They are posted at the front door of nearly every American Embassy throughout the world, the front door of the White House, the side door of the President's Marine One helicopter, and at the front door to the portals wherever our nuclear weapons are deployed at sea. Everyone in the world knows who the Marines are—they epitomize what we want the world to see as the American character. Words like, "duty, honor, country, courage, commitment" are inherent to the Marine culture. Their culture is rooted deep in tradition that dates back even before our country was founded 224 years ago. America's birthday is July 4, 1776; the Marine Corps birthday is November 10, 1775. "First to Fight" is another Marine motto and indeed it is their legacy. Marines were there when Washington crossed the Delaware and when John Paul Jones stormed the British frigate Serapes after his famous words, "I have not yet begun to fight." And they were there in 1995, 224 years later to rescue downed Air Force pilot Scott O'Grady over Bosnia.

Ask any former Marine if he believes in "once a Marine, always a Marine," and they always answer yes. I have seen "Semper Fidelis" inked on the back of helmets and flak jackets, stuck on bumper stickers and pickup truck windows, and even tattoos. It is displayed by "the Few and the Proud." Semper Fi is part of their character, and serves many as a battle dressing to cover the gash on a warrior's heart.

When you see Marines in their working clothes, you don't see their uniforms lavishly decorated with gold epaulets, gold ropes and belts, with gold insignias. Other than their personal combat decorations, their uniform insignias are black. Their "red badge of courage" is their history.

The scarlet red stripe you see on the dress blue uniform of a Marine is there as a remembrance of the blood shed by Marines at the fortress of Chapultepec, Mexico, at the "Halls of Montezuma." There too, the Marine Corps Hymn was born. The sword you see carried by Marines in ceremony is there as a tribute. It was presented to the 20-year-old Lieutenant O'Bannon for a daring attack in defeating the Barbary Pirates on "the shores of Tripoli," and commemorates that event.

That scarlet red stripe never fades; it just turns a deeper red, enriched by sacrifice and character. Immortal phrases like "uncommon valor was a common virtue" don't come cheap. Marines paid a heavy price for the glory bestowed by such phrases. These words are engraved on the statue of the Marines planting our flag on top of Mount Suribachi, Iwo Jima. More than six thousand Marines lost their lives planting that flag—including three of the six pictured. Twenty-four won the Medal of Honor—more Medals of Honor were awarded than in any other battle in history, half of them posthumously. Leathernecks or Devil Dogs, to us they are our Marines. They are our warriors. Theirs is a creed built by their character. It is their sword, honed to the sharpened edge by "duty, honor, courage, trust" in each other and "Semper Fidelis."

TR wrote:

"No qualities called out by a purely peaceful life stand to a level with those stern and virile virtues which move the men of stout heart and strong hand who uphold the honor of their flag in battle."

MUDDY WATER

Into the depths of character analysis, the waters can run muddy. If we dredge the mud in search of character, perhaps an oyster will surface, maybe even a pearl. The character of a Presidency would be dredged through the mud in 1972, but few oysters surfaced. One pearl. The event is known in history as "Watergate."

It began with a third-rate burglary in the offices of the Democratic National Committee headquarters at the Watergate office building in Washington, D.C. It culminated in 1974, with the resignation of our President Richard Nixon. The President of the United States had to resign from office because of criminal wrongdoing resulting from lying to the American people. More than a dozen people were indicted for crimes ranging from breaking and entering to obstruction of justice. Most of them were sentenced to brief prison terms. John Dean, Special Counsel to the President, received the most lenient sentence for his cooperation with the government and served four months. G. Gordon Liddy, the person in charge of the burglary was sentenced to 20 years.

Liddy was charged with several counts of breaking the law connected with the actual burglary including burglary, intercepting wire communications, intercepting an oral communication, and conspiracy to do all of the above. The judge sentenced Liddy to prison for 20 years, not for those crimes, but for contempt of court because Liddy refused to testify either against himself or anyone else, but nor would he lie! The Fifth Amendment protected him from self-incrimination but not from testifying against others. In time, he would be brought before Senator Sam Irvin's committee and asked, "Do you solemnly swear to tell the truth, the whole truth, and nothing but the truth so help you God?" Liddy's reply, "I do not." He was sent back to jail.

Even though Liddy was wrong in breaking the law, his character surfaces through the mud for several reasons. In his life Liddy took the Oath of Conduct and Oath of Office three times, once as an officer in the U.S Army, once as an agent for the Federal Bureau of Investigation, and again as a prosecutor for the District Attorney's Office. He knew full well the law and the Constitution. When he chose to break the law, he also consciously chose to pay the price. He never entered a plea of not guilty and never attempted to mitigate his situation by pointing a finger at others. He took full responsibility for his own actions and stood solely accountable and guilty before the law, choosing to serve his sentence. Liddy spent a total of four years in prison. He compromised on the law but not his principles and paid his debt to society in the process.

On April 12, 1977, President Jimmy Carter commuted Liddy's sentence "in the interests of justice."

The Great Adventure--Untold

On September 1980 Liddy was inducted into the "Honor Legion" of the Police Department of the City of New York. Later he was invited to the United States Military Academy at West Point where he addressed the senior class of the Corps of Cadets, and where he was presented with one of his most prized possessions—a cased cadet officer's sword. Following that, the National Association of Radio Talk Show Hosts (his peers) presented their highest award—the Freedom of Speech Award. Aside from these awards, Liddy is most proud of his children, four of the five served with honor as officers in the United States military. His second most prized possession is a 1911 Colt 45, Officer's model, with handles made of pearl.

While TR was not one to compromise on matters of law, he did, however, leave room for reform and compassion. He wrote:

"Surely every one of us who knows his own heart must know that he too may stumble, and should be anxious to help his brother or sister who has stumbled. When the criminal has been punished, if he then shows a sincere desire to lead a decent and upright life, he should be given the chance he should be helped and not hindered."

Mistakes

Theodore Roosevelt's Cousin Franklin Roosevelt, our 32nd President, made the following statement during his first inaugural address:

> *"This is preeminently the time to speak the truth, the whole truth, frankly and boldly . . . . So, first of all, let me assert my firm belief that the only thing we have to fear is fear itself."*

Fear and the fear of failure stifle the development of character. If character rises from the decisions we make between right and wrong, then we should not fear mistakes, for mistakes are a certainty. The more choices we make, the greater the opportunity for mistakes. But with choice also comes a greater opportunity to hone one's character. The success of the process lies in the foundation of our choices. If the decision we make is anchored in a righteous, moral and ethical foundation, should a mistake occur in that process, it is much easier to repair. On the other hand, if our decision is rooted in a sinister, unethical, immoral plot of deceit or disingenuous statement, should it fail, it probably cannot be corrected.

President Ronald Reagan sent Marine "Peacekeepers" to Beirut, Lebanon, on a mission of peace. On October 23, 1983, at 6:22 in the morning, an Iranian suicide bomber drove a five-ton truck loaded with 12,000 pounds of TNT through a marine barricade and crashed it into the marine barracks. It exploded and killed 220 Marines, 18 Navy corpsmen and three soldiers. More Marines died that Sunday morning than any single day since D-Day on Iwo Jima. President Reagan came before the American people on TV and said that it was his fault and that he took full responsibility for what happened. The American people had been deeply saddened, but impressed with his admission of executive failure and responsibility. They trusted in him. They empathized with him and understood the burden he faced, and they sympathized with the families. He had made a terrible mistake. It was his fault. He had the authority and made the decision to deploy the so called "Peacekeepers." As Commander in Chief he also had the responsibility to see to the security of our troops placed in harm's way. He failed and Marine Corps security failed. But the American people, through their trust, supported President Reagan and their Marines. His decision to supply personnel in concert with the French and Italian governments was rooted in the moral belief that it was the right thing to do. Perhaps it wasn't! The people of Lebanon were not ready for peace —they still had some killing to do. Before the Peacekeepers would be pulled out, 58 French paratroopers, another 25 U.S. Marines, two Italian soldiers, and 62 civilian employees of the U.S. Embassy, 17 of which were American, would die from acts of suicide bombers.

President Reagan visited and consoled the families of every American who died, then brought the Peacekeepers home.

Theodore Roosevelt wasn't afraid of mistakes. He believed in the challenge of what he called "the strenuous life," a life of constant pursuit of endeavor, noble cause, and making choices.

"It is not the critic who counts, not the man who points out how the strong man stumbled or where the doer of deeds could have done better. The credit belongs to the man who is actually in the arena; whose face is marred by dust and sweat and blood; who errs and comes short again . . . who knows the great enthusiasms, the great devotions, and spends himself in a worthy cause; who at least knows in the end the triumph of high achievement; and who, at worst, if he fails, at least fails while doing greatly, so that his place shall never be with those cold and timid souls who know neither victory nor defeat."

Roosevelt's favorite heroes were George Washington and Abraham Lincoln. Both men made a lot of choices between right and wrong, and, in the process, mistakes. Roosevelt frequently cites Lincoln in his political writings. Remember, Lincoln, a man with little formal education, would deliver the most profound writings in American history. But "Honest Abe" did make a lot of mistakes in his pursuit of the strenuous life.

Abraham Lincoln tried practically every job there was—farmer, rail splitter, store clerk, captain of the militia in the Black Hawk War, postmaster, surveyor, newspaper subscription agent, operator of a whiskey still, Mississippi River flatboat hand. He even went into a partnership in the retail business that subsequently failed. But he did become a very successful lawyer. He also ran for a host of political offices beginning with state legislative offices, to U.S. Congress and the Senate. He lost about as many elections as he won. But he did become President of the United States. Lincoln's challenges of triumph and defeat in life were many. He and Mary Lincoln had four children. Sadly, three of them died before adulthood. As Commander in Chief, he faced the most awesome burden of any President in our history. Unlike Washington, Lincoln commanded an army whose enemy was us, remember, Americans killing Americans. He almost lost. And probably would have if it were not for the overwhelming superiority of the North's manpower and materiel. Initially, Lincoln asked Robert E. Lee to command the Union Army. Lee respectfully refused saying, *"I cannot draw my sword against my native state."* Ultimately, Lincoln had to replace five commanding generals before settling on Ulysses S. Grant, our 18th President. Abe Lincoln was a man of many mistakes, but he became our greatest President.

TR relied heavily on Lincoln for guidance throughout his life:

"Lincoln is my hero. He was a man of the people who always felt with and for the people, but who had not the slightest touch of demagogue in him."

Charles Hamman

Honest Abe and TR had plenty in common—particularly, they both understood the price of freedom.

This is evident in Lincoln's letter to the heartbroken mother who lost five sons in the Civil War:

"Dear Madam, —I have been shown, in the files of the War Department, a statement of the Adjutant-General of Massachusetts, that you are the mother of five sons who have died gloriously on the field of battle. I feel how weak and fruitless must be any words of mine which should attempt to beguile you from the grief of a loss so overwhelming. But I cannot refrain from tendering to the consolation that may be found in the thanks of the republic they died to save. I pray that our Heavenly Father may assuage the anguish of your bereavement, and leave you only cherished memory of the loved and lost and the solemn pride that must be yours to have laid so costly a sacrifice upon the altar of freedom."

Yours Very Sincerely and Respectfully,
Abraham Lincoln

A MOUNTAIN OF CHARACTER

Honesty and truthfulness were the foundations for Theodore Roosevelt's character and paramount to everything else. On these two subjects he offered the following.

Honesty:

"We can as little afford to tolerate a dishonest man in the public service as a coward in the army . . . . We can afford to differ on the currency, the tariff, and foreign policy; but we cannot afford to differ on the question of honesty if we expect our republic permanently to endure. No community is healthy where it is ever necessary to distinguish one politician among his fellows because 'he is honest.' Honesty is not so much a credit as an absolute prerequisite to efficient service to the public. Unless a man is honest we have no right to keep him in public life, it matters not how brilliant his capacity, it hardly matters how great his power of doing good service on certain lines may be."

Truthfulness:

"Be truthful; a lie implies fear, vanity, or malevolence; be frank; furtiveness and insincerity are faults incompatible with true manliness. Be honest, and remember that honesty counts for nothing unless back of it lie courage and efficiency.

'Liar' is just as ugly a word as 'thief,' because it implies the presence of just as ugly a sin in one case as in the other. If a man lies under oath or procures the lie of another under oath, if he perjures himself or suborns perjury, he is guilty under the statute law. Under the higher law, under the great law of morality and righteousness, he is precisely as guilty if, instead of lying in a court, he lies in a newspaper or on the stump; and in all probability the evil effects of his conduct are infinitely more widespread and more

pernicious. The difference between perjury and mendacity is not in the least one of morals or ethics. It is simply one of legal forms."

Theodore Roosevelt's character shined through in everything that he wrote, said, or did. In fact, it was his enormous character that put him on Mt. Rushmore. I was 14 years old when I read my first book about "Teddy Roosevelt and the Rough Riders." I wondered how does a kid grow up in New York City, become a cowboy and a famous hunter, then lead a cavalry charge up San Juan Hill, become President of the United States, and wind up on Mt. Rushmore? I concluded that just being an American wasn't enough—it took an American with a "mountain" of character. It is my opinion that if George Washington was our most beloved President, and Abraham Lincoln was our greatest President, then Theodore Roosevelt was our most extraordinary President. He was the last President to have a bigger than life statue made in his honor, riding so proudly on his war horse "Little Texas." And he was the first President to drive a car. He was also the first President to go up in an airplane, and then dive in a submarine. He was a man of many firsts, and he definitely did not believe in second place in anything. Theodore Roosevelt carried America into the 20th century on the back of his character.

Theodore Roosevelt was born on October 27, 1858, at the family house, No. 28 on East Twentieth Street, New York City. His father Theodore Roosevelt Sr. was of Dutch ancestry. His family dated back to the Pilgrims and had arrived in America about 1644.

Some even came over with William Penn. TR's mother Martha Bulloch was of Scottish ancestry. Her great grandfather was Archibald Bulloch, the first Revolutionary "President" of Georgia. They were southerners. They were southerners, and the Roosevelt's were "Yankees."

TR was born a sickly child, chronically uncomfortable, and probably should have died by the time he was four. His most serious problem was chronic asthma, which nearly suffocated him. Doctors had little understanding of this illness at the time and no medication. The only thing that saved TR was his father. His father would take TR for long rides in their horse drawn carriage at night when the air was freshest, so young Teddy could breathe. In time, his father told TR, *"Theodore, you have the mind but you have not the body, and without the help of body, the mind cannot go as far as it should."* The only way to overcome his illness was to literally outgrow it; but at the same time he would have to build up his body to combat it. TR did just that and continued a vigorous physical regimen for the rest of his life—all outdoor activities, with the exception of boxing.

Because of his illness he could not attend where he had to compete physically with other kids. Consequently, TR was home schooled by his aunt and tutors. TR's father became his hero, and he credits his father with instilling the foundation for his character.

"My father, Theodore Roosevelt, was the best man I ever knew. He combined strength and courage with gentleness, tender-

ness, and great unselfishness. He would not tolerate in us children selfishness or cruelty, idleness, cowardice, or untruthfulness. As we grew older, he made us understand that the same standard of clean living was demanded for the boys as for the girls; that what was wrong in a woman could not be right in a man. With great love and patience, and the most understanding sympathy and consideration, he combined insistence on discipline . . . ."

One day when young TR was playing in Central Park, two boys roughed him up. They did not hurt him, but they did intimidate him and left him feeling helpless. He told his father about it. Theodore Senior hired a former prizefighter named John Long to teach TR how to box. It took TR a long time to gain ability, but eventually he won a couple of bouts against two other boys. He received a pewter mug as a prize, and it became one of his most cherished possessions. Once while away from home, he wrote the following letter.[2]

"The boxing gloves are a source of great amusement to us. Whenever Johnnie comes to see us we have an hour's boxing or so. Each round takes one or two minutes.
    The best round yet was one yesterday between Johnnie and I. I shall describe it briefly. After some striking and warding, I got Johnnie into a corner, when he sprung out. We each warded off a right hand blow and brought in a left hander. His took effect behind my ear, and for a minute I saw stars and reeled back to the center of the room, while Johnnie had had his nose and upper lip mashed together and been driven back against the door. I was so weak however that I was driven across the room, simply warding off blows, but I almost disabled his left arm, and drove him back to the middle where some sharp boxing occurred. I got in one on his

forehead which raised a bump, but my eye was made black and blue. At this minute 'Up' was called and we had to separate . . . . If you offered rewards for bloody noses you would spend a fortune on me alone. All send love."

TR would box for the rest of his physically active life, including much of his seven years in the White House. He had a boxing ring set up in the White House gym and would invite young Army and Navy officers in for sparring matches. It was during one of these boxing sessions as President that he took a sharp blow to his left eye that ultimately left him blind in that eye. It was probably more the result of a "thumbing;" boxing gloves in those days did not have the padded construction that they have today. It was common knowledge that if you wanted to adjust your negotiating skills prior to entering discussions on matters of State with the President, you could always come over to the White House for a tune up.

TR matured while at Harvard. He was 5'8", 130 pounds, reddish hair. H.W. Brands sites the following account: During his championship fight for the Light Weight Division at Harvard, he took a devastating blow from his opponent—after the bell rang. The crowd booed and cried foul. TR waved the crowd off saying, *"It's all right—he didn't hear,"* then walked over to his opponent, bloody nose and all, and shook his hand. TR lost the title fight but not the admiration of his classmates or the reporter from the Boston Globe. In time people forgot who won the fight, but they did not forget TR and his grand gesture.[3]

Once while serving as New York assemblyman at age of 23, he encountered a confrontation with a fellow assemblyman who was mocking TR's clothes and high-pitched voice. TR knocked him down with one quick jab to the jaw and said, *"When you sir are in the presence of gentlemen, conduct yourself as a gentleman."* H.W. Brands points out that TR's endorsement to the State Assembly came with a signed statement from party notables affirming their appreciation of Roosevelt's "high character and standing in the community and their confidence in his honesty and integrity. He was, they declared, eminently qualified to represent the District in the Assembly.

There are, of course, other stories of TR's boxing, but suffice it to say that he honed his character through boxing by learning the values of pride and humility, courage over fear, and that a fight worth fighting was a fight worth winning. Boxing instilled a great confidence in him. Whenever TR encountered adversity in life, he could step into any arena, ready to meet any challenge, and prevail. This winning attitude became the propellant that ignited his political career. He loved a "bully good fight," and people loved a winner.

Following boxing lessons, TR was taught to shoot a gun by his father. TR could not see very well and was never a really good shot. And by his own admission he said, *"I don't shoot very good, but I shoot often."* Incidentally, the last gift TR received from his father was a custom cut double-barreled shotgun. But it was during childhood, in pursuit of physical exercise, hiking in the Adirondacks and the woods of Maine that young TR learned about nature. He would hunt and study the birds and woodland creatures of the forest. At one point as a child he even took lessons from a taxidermist, got certified, and became quite good at it. He filled his room full of birds and critters and documented the characteristics of every animal. He called it the Roosevelt Museum of Natural History. In time he would become in his own right one of our country's great naturalists and our country's greatest conservationist.

When the Civil War broke out, TR's father Theodore Roosevelt Sr. chose not to serve. But it wasn't all by his choice. TR's mother would not stand for Theodore Sr. to go to war against her brothers and family who were fighting for the Confederacy. The Bullochs were fighting on the wrong side of the war, but they did so with conspicuous gallantry. Two of TR's uncles, James Bulloch and Irvine Bulloch, gained so much notoriety in fact that they were excluded from the general amnesty proclamation at the end of the war and were exiled to Great Britain for the horrendous damage they had inflicted upon Union shipping. TR was 11 years old when he first met them while on a trip to England. He idolized his hero uncles, and later in life he convinced them to write their published memoirs, *"The Secret Service of the Confederate States in Europe."*

Theodore Sr.'s brother Barnwell Roosevelt, however, did fight for the Union army, but not Theodore Sr. Instead he bought his way out by paying a broker $1,000 to hire a German immigrant named Abraham Graf to take his place. This was allowed at the time, by law, under the terms of the 1863 Conscription Bill. Theodore Sr., however, served the Union by performing significant services such as a civilian allotment commissioner. It was a service that he created to assist Federal soldiers in setting aside portions of their pay for their families. Later in life Theodore Sr. regretted his decision and considered his conduct less than honorable. He set about to make it right by doing great works as a philanthropist in New York, which deeds are still recognized to this day. TR never spoke about this matter with his father, but he was ashamed and was determined that it would never happen in his life. TR also never found out about Abraham Graf who was captured by the Confederates, imprisoned, and later died of fever and scurvy in a Union hospital at Point Lookout, Maryland. Graf got $38 out of the deal.

Theodore Roosevelt Sr. died in 1878 from cancer. He was 48 years old. TR was only 19 at the time and emotionally devastated. He had lost his father and his best friend at the same time. Theodore Sr. was an extremely moral man and had taught TR his moral code of conduct. He said, *"You should take care of your morals first, health next, then your studies."* And TR had been doing just that—but now without his father's counsel.

TR continued his studies at Harvard and his strict physical workout program. He regularly took eight mile afternoon walks, boat rows of 20-25 miles, horseback rides of 25 to 40 miles, and long hikes, hunting in the Adirondacks and Maine, and a couple of forays to the Dakotas. He was in top physical shape. He even went to Europe and climbed the Matterhorn. During this time, he fell in love with his childhood sweetheart Alice Lee. He was married on his 22nd birthday, Oct 27, 1878. He ran for the New York State Assembly as a Republican and won, and was then re-elected by an enormous majority. He was the youngest man there at 23. With his inheritance money, he bought land at Oyster Bay on Long Island to build a home for his new family, and invested in a cattle operation in the Dakotas. Then tragedy struck again. On Valentine's Day February 14, 1884, while at her bedside, TR watched his mother Mitte die from typhoid fever. Just hours later, upstairs in the same house, his childhood sweetheart Alice Lee died from complications giving birth to their baby daughter two days earlier. TR was just 25 years old.

Once again he was left devastated. He wrote, *"For joy or for sorrow my life has now been lived out."* He named the baby Alice and recruited a volunteer, his sister Bamie, to serve as a surrogate mother. TR was now faced with a critical choice. Although emotionally crushed by his loss, he would choose a path of change and personal challenge over self-pity and set a course to rebuild his spent soul.

The lessons his father had taught him about moral conduct, integrity, and honesty were well entrenched in his character, and they would accompany him in his renewed quest for the American dream. He left politics and New York City for the Badlands of the Dakotas and his Chimney Butte Ranch on the Little Missouri River.

TR wrote in his autobiography, *"If it were not for the time I spent in the West, I would never have become President."* This is a truly profound statement; but in actuality it is a profound understatement. Because of his time in the West, he became much more— a rancher and a cowboy for sure. He owned two ranches, the Chimney Butte Ranch and the Elkhorn Ranch. At first the cowboys were unsure of him. He wore thick glasses, dressed a bit of a dandy, was from New York City, and talked differently. But he had grit, which was obvious. They could out rope him on cattle, but they couldn't out work him. Some of them could break buckin' horses, something TR did not do. But he could ride the rough stock. (Incidentally that is where the term "Rough Rider" comes from.) They could not out ride him across the Badlands nor match his enthusiasm and energetic vigor. The cowboys came to respect him as an honest man, who sought challenge and hard work, who was daring and tenacious in all endeavors. There are many stories about

TR and his cowboy days. The following is one that cemented the bond with his cowboy friends.

TR walked into a hotel/saloon to get a bed and something to eat. A ruffian was there with a gun in each hand and had apparently just shot out the clock. He was drunk and shouting obscenities. He called out, *"Four eyes there is going to treat the house."* Meaning TR was going to buy the house a round of drinks. TR tried to ignore him, but the bully came over to his table, and, standing over TR with a cocked pistol in each hand, started in with more profanity. TR rose from his chair saying, *"Well, if I have to, I have to."* Then, looking past the guy, hit him with a right lead, followed by a left and another straight right hand. The bully was knocked out and hauled off. Word spread about "four-eyes."

Theodore Roosevelt went on to write about his cowboy days in several books and hundreds of magazine articles. It was during this time as a cowboy that his character was honed to a gilt edge.

In time TR left the Badlands, but not the people. The people of the Great Plains and the Rocky Mountain West would remember him forever. They adopted him as one of their own as later witnessed at the ballot box.

TR came to the West already a naturalist in his own right, but he became our nation's most renowned hunter and our greatest conservationist. He became a great hunter not because he killed the biggest trophies, but rather because he educated the American people about their wildlife, which at the time they knew little about. He wrote several books and hundreds of magazine articles on the subject. He did not just write about the sport of hunting, he wrote about hunting from the perspective of a naturalist. His books and stories were much more than entertaining, they were informative and educational.

He wrote about the ways and habits of the woodland creatures and the characteristics of each species. Some people said that only one man in America could name and identify more birds on sight than TR and that was John Audubon himself. Ultimately, TR was sponsored by the Smithsonian Institute to hunt and collect animals for study and display at the American Museum of Natural History. They honored his academic credentials, trusted in his professional ethics, and, above all else, placed total faith in a man who regarded trust as a sacred responsibility.

The most eloquent and best introduction to any book I have ever read, either fiction or non-fiction, was written by Theodore Roosevelt titled *African Game Trails*, where he honors and exalts a people and their land. Later TR started the Boone and Crockett Club, an internationally renowned conservation group dedicated to the preservation of wildlife and habitat. It is still in existence and proactive in conservation efforts today. It was named after TR's two favorite frontier heroes Daniel Boone and David Crockett.

TR counted among his friends America's most famous naturalists, John Muir and John Burroughs. Both helped to guide TR's great accomplishments at conservation. TR created five National Parks (among them Yosemite, The Grand Canyon, and Mesa Verde), 18 National Monuments, 51 bird sanctuaries, 150 National Forests, and set aside 230 million acres under public protection. He also passed the Reclamation Act, which ultimately provided many of the great conservation projects and water playgrounds in the arid west such as Lake Powell and Lake Mead. I have boated on the Theodore Roosevelt Reservoir in Arizona, hiked and hunted the vast Roosevelt National Forest in Colorado, and photographed the buffalo that TR put in Yellowstone.

We the people owe a great debt to Theodore Roosevelt for his foresight in preserving our natural resources. All of this was accomplished because of one of the most regarded field naturalists this country has ever produced, an American hunter who wanted to preserve habitat for wildlife and our natural resources for the American people. TR wrote:

"There can be nothing in the world more beautiful than the Yosemite, the groves of the giant sequoia and redwoods, the Canyon of Colorado, the canyon of the Yellowstone, the three Tetons; and our people should see to it that they are preserved for their children, and their children's children forever, with their majestic beauty all unmarred."

His accomplishments in conservation were not achieved without controversy, but he was a man of vision and principle—country first, special interest second. He relished the challenge, and he knew how to win.

TR became a great author and essayist. He wrote 35 books, all non-fiction, and over 150 thousand magazine and newspaper articles, essays, speeches, and letters. TR was also a voracious reader. He could read and write in several languages and had an encyclopedic mind with mental recall beyond comprehension. It is estimated that Roosevelt's library at one time contained over 12,000 books. To say that TR read them all would not be much of a stretch. The opinions that shaped his political ideology were anchored in the depth of his character and often rooted in historical fact.

He was named President of the National Historical Society. It was not an honorary title; he actually earned it by contributing four volumes titled *The Winning of the West* and several other historical books that received national acclaim.

TR went on to become U.S. Civil Service Commissioner, President of the Police Board of Commissioners of New York City, Assistant Secretary of the Navy, Governor of New York, Vice President, and then President of the United States.

As top cop in New York City, TR stamped out corruption and graft, and turned a corrupt police force into "New York's Finest." He took police graft personally. It offended his sense of justice and even patriotism, not to mention his character. To him it was un-American. There are dozens of accounts where TR would put on disguises and sneak around day and night busting bad cops. But at the same time he also lavished praise on good cops. He established the first police academy in the United States with a nationally accredited pistol school. He also established the Bureau of Investigation, the forerunner to the FBI.

TR was unyielding on matters of the law and uncompromising on principles governing the conduct of public officials. He wrote,

"The greatest benefit to the people, I am convinced, is the enforcement of the laws, without fear or favor . . . .

No man is above the law and no man is below it; nor do we ask any man's permission when we require him to obey it . . . .

Our cause is the cause of justice for all in the interest of all."

Later in life he took on big business monopolies with anti-trust laws, established the Pure Food and Drug Act, set standards for child labor laws, and championed women's rights. He preached the "square deal," (fair treatment and fair representation of service for the citizen), and kicked in the door of injustice wherever he saw it. To TR there was no gray area between right and wrong. He preached about "the strenuous life." *" . . . I wish not to preach, not the doctrine of ignoble ease, but the doctrine of the strenuous life, the life of toil and effort, of labor and strife, to preach that highest form of success which comes, not to the man who desires mere easy peace, but to the man who does not shrink from danger, from hardship, or from bitter toil, and who out of these wins the splendid ultimate triumph."* This is the character of a man whose overwhelming ebullience for everything in life and indomitable spirit set about a course to build upon the character of a nation.

In 1898 America declared war on Spain, and Congress called for a Volunteer Army. TR at 39 years, since remarried to Edith Carow, and with six children at home, resigned as Assistant Secretary of the Navy and accepted a position as a Lieutenant Colonel in the First Volunteer Cavalry, the Rough Riders. In doing so, he also accepted the responsibility for recruitment. He consulted with Edith first, out of loving courtesy of course. Edith acquiesced, knowing full well that TR had to go. There was no choice for him to make where duty and honor were concerned. She also knew that Theodore Sr. had not served when he was called, and she knew full well that weighed heavily on TR. It was his duty; his country was calling for brave men, and he was going to serve. The Rough Riders were recruited out of San Antonio, Texas, beneath the shadow of the Alamo. More that 23,000 men applied, but only 1,000 were accepted. They were the cream of the crop. TR wrote that his biggest burden was not in finding brave and hardy men to fill the ranks, but, rather, the burden was in rejecting the thousands of other brave men. The majority of the recruits were cowboys, miners, ranchers, Indians, and tough, self-reliant adventurous men from all over the southwest. But also included were 200 Ivy League athletes from Yale, Harvard, Princeton, and Columbia—Hamilton Fish (Team Captain at Columbia and a millionaire), Allyn Capron of Ft. Sill, Oklahoma, (fifth generation of American warriors who served in five consecutive wars), and Bucky O'Neil (Mayor of Prescott, Arizona, sheriff, and famous Indian fighter). And William Tiffany of the famous Tiffany's jewelry store in New York City. These men were all killed before the charge up Kettle Hill.

Fighting beside TR and his Rough Riders were the Buffalo Soldiers, black troops of the 9th and 10th Cavalry commanded by First Lieutenant John "Black Jack" Pershing. They were professional Army Cavalry.

The Rough Riders and Buffalo Soldiers were pinned down and taking casualties from cannon shrapnel and Spanish Mausers. Somebody had to take charge and then—*CHARGE!*

TR led the charge up Kettle Hill, initially on horseback, riding "Little Texas." He described it as his "crowded hour." He was grazed by two bullets, one in the boot the other on the elbow. Eventually he was forced to dismount and charge on foot because of barbed wire and continued to lead the charge on foot all the way to San Juan Hill. His Rough Riders sustained 23 percent casualties, the heaviest casualties in the regiment. The historical record is clear—

that without his leadership, initiative, and fearless courage, the assault would have failed and additional casualties would have been probable. Pershing took note of TR's fearless leadership in the field and described it as "indispensable" to the day's success.[6] The commanding field general and ex-Confederate cavalry hero "Fighting" Joe Wheeler put TR in for the Medal of Honor. Others in the command staff recognized TR's heroics and endorsed the nomination. The only other Medals of Honor went to the Buffalo Soldiers, and deservedly so.

Following the battle, a controversy erupted. The U.S. War Department, then headed by Secretary of War Russell Alger, decided to leave the troops in Cuba for awhile. The men were dying of malaria, typhoid fever, and the beginning stages of yellow fever. The command staff (by vote) selected TR to write a report in the form of a letter to the Secretary of War demanding extradition of the troops back to the mainland before they all died. TR eagerly obliged. It was referred to as a round robin letter, and all of the officers signed it. Somehow the letter found its way to the press. The American people became outraged, the Administration was embarrassed, and Russell Alger almost had to resign. They brought the Army home. But the Secretary of War shelved TR's Medal of Honor. In essence, the Administration denied it.

In 1997 Congressman Paul McHale, a former Marine, submitted a bill to Congress to get TR his medal. In 1998 the House and Senate together passed the bill by a unanimous vote. The President signed it and sent it to the Army for review and report. TR got his Medal of Honor!

TR made it clear that he felt he deserved the Medal of Honor. However, it is interesting to note that once he became President of the United States, he did not use the influence of his office to secure the medal for himself. His personal pride and honor would not allow it. In truth he would never have done anything different. The words he wrote, he meant. Those were his troops. He would have died for them; and they would have died for him. They were blood brothers, "children of the dragon's blood" as he put it, and "first to fight." The Rough Riders revered his leadership, his courage, and his character. Later, they paraded him into the office of the Presidency, and they were there at his funeral—Always faithful —Semper Fi.

TR wrote,

"The fighting has been very hard. I don't know whether people at home know how well this regiment did. I am as proud of it as I can be . . . . This is a regiment of Crackerjacks—American from start to finish—in the best and fullest sense of the term."

In 1900 TR was elected Vice President of the United States with William McKinley as President. Seven months later McKinley was assassinated and TR became President. He was 42 years old, the youngest President in U.S. history. TR's first day in office was coincidentally his father's birthday. TR spent two terms in office before voluntarily stepping aside. He did so in the spirit of George Washington, who also had refused a 3rd term. In time TR became one of the most popular and respected man in the world, and this was later obvious when he attended the funeral of Britain's King Edward VII. During the funeral procession, the world media focused all cameras on King Edward's horse drawn carriage and then on Theodore Roosevelt the former American President who was now just an American citizen walking at the very back of the procession. When TR returned to the United States, he received the biggest ticker tape parade ever in the history of New York City.

TR believed that a strong navy was necessary to project power and preserve the peace. He put together a huge group of battle ships and had those all painted white. It was called "The Great White Fleet." He then sent them on a mission to circumnavigate the globe. It was the first time in world history that such a feat had ever been attempted and accomplished by a naval armada. It also sent a message to the world that "America had arrived." At the same time he saw the need for the Panama Canal so he could effectively move this navy. So he built it! The French actually had started it, but they failed. TR didn't. America would build the canal. In doing so TR sent another message to the world that the U.S. was not going to tolerate interference in affairs in the western hemisphere, the Canal included. He invoked the Monroe Doctrine and preached a policy of "Walk softly and carry a big stick." When he was fighting the big U.S. corporate monopolies, using the anti-trust laws, and then the mandate he carried from the American people became his "big stick." To the Europeans and others who had their eyes on intervention and interference in our backyard, the Monroe Doctrine and the U.S. Navy was his big stick

In 1906 he was awarded the Nobel Peace Prize for brokering a peace deal between two warring nations—the Russians and the Japanese. TR possessed the character demanded by such a challenge. At one point he was so mad at the Russians for lying and the Japanese for being nonnegotiable that he said:

"I am so mad at them that I could jump up and bash their heads together—but I doubt it should be good for my character."

It is interesting to note that in receiving the Medal of Honor, he is the only person in history to have received the Nobel Peace Prize and his country's highest military award for conspicuous bravery in battle.

In 1912 TR was campaigning for the Presidency again, this time as a third party candidate under the Bull Moose Party. He believed that the Taft administration had become inept and he was therefore duty bound to step forward and restore good government. On October 14, while campaigning in Milwaukee, TR was shot in the chest by John Schank with a 38 caliber revolver. Shank had been stalking TR and finally found his opportunity. The bullet passed through TR's jacket and vest but was drastically slowed as it passed through a 50 page speech that had been folded over and stuck in his jacket pocket. The bullet also went through a metal eye glass case which caused a deflection, resulting in the slug ricocheting off of a rib then coming to rest between the rib and lung. It did not penetrate the lung. TR was knocked down, but rose to his feet crippled and holding his chest. The assassin was subdued and the crowd was going to beat the assassin to death. TR intervened saying that no harm should come to the man and that he should be accorded due process of law. In the meantime a couple of doctors came to TR's aid and demanded he be evacuated immediately. He refused, saying emphatically that he came to give a speech and he was going to give it. He stated that since he wasn't coughing blood, the wound wasn't fatal. He asked the crowd for calm and then said:

"I don't know whether you fully understand that I have just been shot; but it takes more than that to kill a Bull Moose. The bullet is in me now, so that I cannot make a very long speech, but I will try my best."

The doctors had applied a compression bandage to stop the bleeding. Then seeing him fade, they begged him to stop—he refused. Turning to the audience, TR said:

"My friends are a little more nervous than I am. Don't you waste any sympathy on me. I have had an A-1 time in life and I am

having it now . . . . I have altogether too important things to think of to feel any concern over my own death; and now I cannot speak to you insincerely within five minutes of being shot. I am telling you the literal truth when I say that my concern is for many other things. It is not in the least my own life."

Indeed it wasn't. This was a man staring destiny in the face—with resolute courage—a man who challenged fate in a bully good fight. A man content with his character, who had done what's right—"when nobody was looking," and everybody was looking—a man with few regrets from yesterday and no regrets on this day, not even after being shot! TR carried that bullet in his chest to his grave.

Theodore Roosevelt, above all else, was a family man and devoted father. Together he and Edith had five children: four boys, Theodore, Archie, Kermit, Quentin, and one girl—Ethel. With his daughter Alice from his first marriage, TR and Edith raised six children.

TR wrote:

"For unflagging interest and enjoyment, a household of children, if things go reasonably well, certainly makes all other forms of success and achievements lose their importance by comparison."

TR built a family home on the property at Oyster Bay and called it Sagamore Hill. Today Sagamore Hill is a National Park managed by the National Park Service and the Theodore Roosevelt

Association. Visitors come from all over the world. On my tour, I saw a large Victorian house in a farm-like setting overlooking Oyster Bay with lots of rooms for kids, guests, and domestic help. There are also many museum quality taxidermy pieces, gifts, and mementos from kings, emperors, presidents, and of course thousands of books. On one wall in TR's study are portraits of George Washington and Abraham Lincoln. Between them hangs a portrait of his father Theodore Sr. Sagamore Hill was a wonderful place to raise children, and it also served later as TR's Presidential retreat.

Horseback riding was the main form of recreation, with each family member having his or her own horse. There was a lot of family bonding done, and more than a few bones broken. In fact, Edith almost died from one horse wreck. Throughout his life TR suffered approximately 20 broken or fractured bones, most the result of horse wrecks. But they kept on riding.

Of Sagamore Hill and family life TR wrote:

"At Sagamore Hill we love a great many things—birds and trees and books, and all things beautiful, and horses and rifles and children and hard work and the joy of life."

All of the kids had pets including bear cubs, raccoons, snakes and critters of all kinds. There were lion rugs and bear rugs in the trophy room, and TR would drape the lion rugs over himself and chase the kids around the house. Eventually they moved into the

White House. The term "White House" incidentally was coined by TR. The kids became known affectionately as the "White House gang."[7] The nation had never seen anything like this before. TR might as well have brought Sagamore Hill with him because the gang did. There are plenty of stories about kids bursting into cabinet meetings pulling critters out of pockets and placing them on the conference room table to the amusement of everyone. There is even one story of two of the boys sneaking their pony into the elevator where they managed to get it passed Secret Service and up to the second floor.[8]

Perhaps the best illustration of TR's devotion to family resides in the letters he wrote to his children. They were eloquently written with love, admiration, wise counsel, and just plain fun. It did not matter if the children were three years old or 30 years old—they got letters. So profound was the impact of his letters that they were compiled in a book titled *Theodore Roosevelt's Letters to His Children*. It made the national best seller's list.

The following example is an excerpt from a letter to his son Ted Jr.

"I am delighted to have you play football. I believe in rough, manly sports. But I do not believe in them if they degenerate into the sole end of any one's existence. I do not want you to sacrifice standing well in your studies to any over-athleticism; and I need not tell you that character for a great deal more than either intellect or body in winning success in life."

This sports metaphor became one of TR's favorites, and he enjoyed sharing it with young people:

"In life, as in a football game, the principle to follow is: hit the line hard; don't foul and don't shirk, but hit the line hard."

TR made it clear that he was taught the value of character from his best friend—his father. He saw to it that his children were taught the same.

In 1913 at the age of 55, TR turned explorer. He wrote a fascinating book titled *Through the Brazilian Wilderness*. It chronicled a harrowing expedition of explorers trekking through the Amazon jungle attempting to map an unknown river, as translated "the river of doubt." His party traveled by canoe for two months and covered 750 kilometers. TR came close to death and should have died. In fact on several occasions he volunteered to stay behind, alone, and wait death.

The American Museum of Natural History and the Brazilian government sponsored the expedition. Kermit, TR's son and hunting partner was along. They had spent 11 months together hunting in Africa, a trip sponsored by the Smithsonian Institute. Also along were a couple of naturalists, two scientists, a doctor, and a small group of Brazil's version of the Army Corps of Engineers. In command were Brazil's Colonel Rondon and military staff. The unexplored river turned into a nightmare. At one point, the canoe Kermit was in flipped over and the guy with him died. Kermit barely made it to safety. Trying to save men in another wrecked canoe, TR jumped into the river. He was busted up good when his leg slammed against a rock, aggravating an old wound he had received from a horse carriage wreck. It became inflamed, with fever and concern about poisonous gangrene became a reality. On top of that, he had recurring bouts of malaria—a gift from the Cuba campaign. Supplies of food and medicine were all but gone, swept overboard; TR was fast losing weight. One of the soldiers went insane and killed a fellow soldier. The killer was banished to the wilderness by Colonel Rondon and left to die. The party continued down the river, with TR horizontal in the bottom of a canoe or portaged on a stretcher. The remaining members of the group survived and the expedition was concluded.

TR tendered the necessary scientific documents, and to the Brazilian government he presented a letter that in essence thanked them for the opportunity to serve, ". . . in this great work of exploration."[9] The Brazilian government renamed the Rio da Duvida, or River of Doubt, the "Rio Roosevelt."

From scholar to explorer, family man to statesman war hero to Nobel Prize winner, and cowboy to President—these were but stepping stones of white granite to the top of the mountain of character.

THE LEGACY

In April 1917, the United States declared war on Germany and the Central Powers. The Allies were in desperate shape, and America did not have an army ready to fight. For months prior to that, TR had petitioned President Wilson and the Secretary of War to give him an opportunity to raise an army of volunteers; he called it the "Roosevelt Division." He proposed to personally lead the army into France to save the Allies. By this time the French and the British had lost in excess of a million men each. TR was eight years beyond his Presidency and 58 years old. Still he would write more than a dozen pieces of eloquent correspondence literally begging the Wilson administration for the opportunity to serve. Some of his letters were very lengthy, spelling out exactly how he would go about creating this rapid deployment of volunteers. He even included the names of officers that had pledged their commitment to the war effort and him and the fact that tens of thousands would volunteer.[10] He would train them in France and have them ready to fight in 90 days. He even met privately with President Wilson. The Leaders of France and England begged President Wilson to send the "Roosevelt Division" as a symbol of American intervention. The Premier of France Georges Clemenceau said in effect that one American in particular could raise the morale of the French soldiers more than any other. "Send Roosevelt."[11] TR informed a confidant that,

> *"If I should die tomorrow, I would be more than content to have as my epitaph, and my only epitaph, Roosevelt to France."*

TR believed that the Germans not only had to be stopped, but put out of commission for good.

TR believed that the Roosevelt Division commanded by him and serving under General Pershing could stop the Kaiser's army. Millions of Americans believed it also and so did the French and the British. President Woodrow Wilson denied TR's request.

TR's sons, however, would not be denied. Like their father before them, there was no choice to make where duty and honor were concerned. They not only wanted to get into the war, but they wanted to get to the front lines and be "the first to fight." TR began calling up political favors and "strong arming" where necessary. First he wrote General "Black Jack" Pershing, who would lead the American expeditionary force.

> *"I write to you now to request that my two sons, Theodore Roosevelt, Jr., age 27, and Archibald B. Roosevelt, aged 23, both of Harvard, be allowed to enlist as privates under you . . . . The former is a Major and the latter is a Captain in the Officers Reserve Corps. P.S. If I were physically fit, instead of old and stiff, I should myself ask to go under you in any capacity . . . ."*

Pershing could not say no—he owed TR.[12] They served in Cuba together and later when TR became President, he promoted Pershing over 862 officers senior to him to Brigadier General. Pershing got the boys in. With their training in the Reserves, Ted was commissioned a Major and Archie a First Lieutenant. They shipped out on the very first transport. Next came Kermit, 26 years old. He too was in the Reserves and upon discharge was recommended for a Captain in the U.S. Army. Kermit, however, did not believe that he could get to the front lines quickly enough to see combat with the American army. So he asked TR to get him into the British army as a quicker route to the front. TR wrote British Prime Minister Lloyd George, *"I pledge my honor that he will serve you honorably and efficiently."* Kermit sailed to England to pick up his commission and then on to the Middle East to fight the Turks in Iraq. Finally, at 20 years old, it was young Quentin's turn. He had been enrolled in a flight training school and, like his brothers, went through Harvard coupled with two summers of ROTC-type training. He sailed for France on July 23 and would complete flight training there, pick up his commission and assignment with the "Kicking Mule" squadron of the First Pursuit Group, 95th Aero Squadron and home of American Ace Eddie Rickenbacker.[13] The sons of Teddy Roosevelt were now overseas. His daughter, her husband, and TR's daughter-in-law would follow.

TR's daughter Ethel signed on as a nurse with her husband Dick Derby, who served as an Army surgeon. Ted Jr.'s wife Eleanor signed up with a YMCA group (forerunner to the USO of WWII). She and Ted Jr. had three children whom they left in the care of Eleanor's mother.

These were the sons and daughters of "the Lion's Pride," as described in Edward Renehan's book titled *The Lion's Pride.* They were posted all along the Western Front—and up front. They were there to "hit the line hard." TR's only regret was that he was not standing shoulder to shoulder with his sons on the "fighting line" as he would say. If he would have one more son, he would have gotten him into his beloved Navy to chase the Germans from the high seas. His sons stood in sharp contrast to the sons of the Kaiser or President Wilson's son-in-law, who joined as volunteer with the YMCA and was to serve with TR's daughter-in-law Eleanor. It became quite an embarrassment for the Wilson administration. The "embarrassment" was sent to a remote soft spot on the Italian frontier—away from reporters. Eleanor was put in charge of all "Y" women volunteers in Paris.[14] While TR's boys were fighting with bayonets and bullets, TR was fighting with words and speeches. He wreaked havoc on the Wilson administration and its unpreparedness to fight war and its lack of resolve to conclude war—quickly and unconditionally. He was most effective.

It wasn't long before TR received word that Archie was severely wounded by flying shrapnel that shattered his knee and severed a main nerve in his arm, leaving him partially paralyzed but alive. He would spend four months in a Paris hospital. He had also been decorated by the American army as well as the French army, having received the French Croix de Guerre. Eleanor attended to him while at the hospital in Paris. Ultimately, Archie with multiple Purple Heart medals would receive a one-hundred percent disability discharge.

Not long after, word got back to Sagamore Hill that Kermit had just received the British War Cross for gallantry in command of a light armored unit at Tikrit, Iraq. After fighting off an assault, he captured a Turkish army group. TR wrote General March, Chief of Staff, to see if he could get Kermit transferred to the American army in France. General March obliged. Kermit would go on to further distinguish himself as an artillery officer throughout the remainder of the war.

On July 16, 1918, word came to TR at Sagamore Hill that Quentin had been shot down over France. It was not known if he was dead or alive. On the fateful day of July 14, Bastille Day in France, Quentin and an outnumbered fighter group of "Kicking Mules" were flying low in an attempt to evade a squadron of German fighter planes in hot pursuit. It was not just another German fighter group—these were warriors of the famed "flying circus." On this day they were commanded by Hermann Goring, a brother in arms to the Red Baron Rittmeister Manfred von Richthofen.[15] Quentin was flying in the rear of his formation when he banked his airplane and returned to intercept the Germans.

There are no American accounts of what happened after that. But Renehan points out that the German government's Wolff Bureau press released a report containing the details. Quentin went back to engage the German squadron, which in effect stopped their pursuit of the Americans. But with one against seven, the outcome was certain. Their report stated that he fought bravely and valiantly.

Quentin made a choice that he did not have to make. And, his choice was no different than that made by Lance Corporal Roy Wheat—they made the "supreme sacrifice." One fact, however, rises above the rest. Quentin was all alone in his "crowded hour" as he faced his destiny with high and resolute courage.

The news was confirmed. TR and Edith had anticipated the unthinkable, but it did not ease their grief. Edith would be the one to rally support within the family and support for TR. Speaking to others close to the Roosevelts, Edith said, *"We must do everything we can to help him,"* referring to TR. *"The burden must not rest entirely on his shoulders."*[16]

TR, left devastated again by the face of death and crushed by emotion, emerged to release a brief statement.

"Quentin's mother and I are very glad that he got to the front and had a chance to render some service to his country, and show the stuff that was in him before fate befell him."

The following morning Edith accompanied TR to a pre-arranged speaking engagement to the New York Republican State Convention. The topic was "speeding up the war." The audience did not know of Quentin's death and TR did not tell them. In his speech he said,

"All of us who give service, and stand ready for sacrifice, are the torch-bearers. We run with the torches until we fall, content if we can pass them to the hands of other runners. The torches whose flame is brightest are borne by the gallant men at the front, and by the gallant women whose husbands and lovers, whose sons and brothers are at the front. These men are high of soul, as they face their fate on the shell-shattered earth, or in the skies above or in the waters beneath; and no less high of soul are the women with torn hearts and shining eyes; the girls whose boy-lovers have been struck down in their golden morning, and the mothers and wives to whom word has been brought that henceforth they must walk in the shadow.

These are the torch-bearers; these are they who have dared the Great Adventure."

In a letter to Archie he wrote,

"And Mother suffers as much and is even braver; for Mother has the true heroism of heart. Well, it is very dreadful; it is the old who ought to die, and not fine and gallant youth with the golden morning of life still ahead; but after all he died as the heroes of old died, as brave and fearless men must die when a great cause calls. If our country did not contain such men it would not be our country. I

bitterly mourn that he was not married and does not leave his own children behind him; but the children's children of his brothers and of Ethel will speak of him with pride as long as our blood flows in the veins of man or woman."

Within days of Quentin's death, word reached Oyster Bay that Ted, Jr., had been wounded. Already once gassed, now he was gunshot. His unit had been in fierce fighting at Chateau-Thierry. Now he lay in a hospital attended by his sister Eleanor and her husband Dick Derby. Ted Jr. was highly decorated for conspicuous bravery, with multiple Silver and Bronze Stars. But for now, his fight was over.

As condolences poured into Sagamore Hill from friends, kings, chancellors, prime ministers, and presidents, so did an anonymous postcard. It was a gruesome picture of Quentin, dead amongst the wreckage of his airplane. The picture was apparently taken by a civilian photographer and found its way to the German press. The Roosevelts did not hide the postcard or hide from it— they were very proud of Quentin and the sacrifice he had made. Nothing would change that. The news of Quentin's death was carried by the international media and was trumpeted in the German press as a victory. But the scheme backfired because it highlighted the stark contrast between the Roosevelt boys and the sons of the Kaiser. The Kaiser had six sons—there were photos of them dressed up lavishly decorated uniforms, like toy soldiers. But they were not soldiers at all, and, if they were serving, they were not serving on the fighting line. The German people were outraged that the Roosevelt boys were fighting all along the front and the Kaiser, who saw fit to send millions of their boys, would not send his own.[17] Dissention rippled throughout the German army ranks.

The Roosevelts had a tradition, "Roosevelts were buried wherever they fell" —like a tree falling in the forest. Quentin was buried outside of Chamery, France, next to the wreckage of his airplane. As advancing American troops moved through the War Theater, many stopped to visit Quentin's grave, so many in fact that they had to rope it off. One soldier was asked why he had come to visit the grave, and he said that he and all of his men felt that they were sons of Teddy Roosevelt and brothers of Quentin.[18]

Another letter of condolences arrived at Sagamore Hill:

"I write these few lines—not of condolence, for who would dare to pity you?—but of deepest sympathy to you and yours as you stand in the shadow which is the earthly side of those clouds of glory in which your son's life has just passed. Many will envy you that when the call to sacrifice came you were not found among the paupers to whom no gift of life worth offering had been entrusted. They are the ones to be pitied, not we whose dearest are jeopardizing their lives unto the death in the high places of the field. I hope my two sons will live as worthily and die as greatly as yours."

On November 11, 1918, WWI, the Great War, the war to end all wars, was over. The Roosevelts had "hit the line hard" with everything they had. They were fearless in battle, selfless in sacrifice, honor bound to duty and country. The character of the

Roosevelts was admired and envied throughout the world. Many countries would name things to honor the Roosevelt family, such as battleships and airfields and points of geography. The character of the Roosevelts represented the highest American ideals.

TR died January 6, 1919. He was 60. He died peacefully in his sleep, from heart failure, at Sagamore Hill. Archie sent out a telegram to family, *"The Old Lion is dead."*

TR was buried in a community cemetery on property adjacent to Sagamore Hill, Oyster Bay, New York. The funeral was simple and private, with Rough Riders serving as honor guard. In one of TR's final passages, he wrote:

"Only those are fit to live who do not fear to die, and none are fit to die who have shrunk from the joy of life and the duty of life. Both life and death are parts of the same Great Adventure."

TR had vigorously preached on the preparedness of peace, the accelerated prosecution of the war, and the destruction of Germany's war machine. President Wilson had pursued a different course. In establishing the Armistice, he concocted a 14-point criterion for Germany's so-called unconditional surrender, which later was concluded at the Treaty of Versailles. Twenty-one years later in 1939 the German army in a blitzkrieg invaded Poland. World War II was now underway and America would soon be called to arms. This time more than five times as many Americans and 20 times as many Europeans would die. But "the Lion's Pride" would again be among the first to fight.

They were all older now, financially successful, married, and with children and grandchildren at home. However, to get into the war, they would have to literally break in. And they did! Our country was calling for brave men. It was something reminiscent of Colonel Crockett and the volunteers breaking into the Alamo.

Ted Jr. went straight to the Army Chief of Staff General George Marshall and asked the General to reinstate him to active duty. Colonel Theodore Roosevelt, Jr., now 54 years old, was given command of his old unit, the 26th Infantry of the First Division.[19]

Kermit, now 50 years old, was in England at the time and not in the best of health. He had been very successful financially, was widely traveled, and had lots of influential friends, including Winston Churchill whom he contacted directly. He negotiated himself a commission in the British army.[20]

Archie was 42 and still troubled by the wounds that led to his 100 percent disability discharge following WWI. To get into this war and get to the front was going to take some serious political pressure. So Archie called on his cousin President Franklin Delano Roosevelt. Archie wrote,[21]

"There may come many places and many times where you would like to have the son of the former President and someone with your name to share the dangers of soldiers or marines in some

tough spot . . . I would be perfect for such a job . . . . You would not be throwing away someone who was useful elsewhere."[22]

Archie was commissioned a Lieutenant Colonel, US Army, and 162nd Infantry.

Kermit was battling the Germans in Norway and found himself caught in a disaster. The British were outgunned, out manned, and out fought. Kermit's unit was forced to retreat and evacuate. Despite deteriorating health, he served with valor once again. But eventually Kermit was unable to overcome his own debilitating heath problems. With help from President Franklin Roosevelt, he was transferred to the American army and posted at Fort Richardson in the Aleutian Islands off of Alaska. His health continued to deteriorate, and, finally overtaken by mental anguish, he concluded his service with a self-inflicted gunshot to the head.[23]

Archie's unit was serving in conjunction with the Australian army trying to push the Japanese out of Nassau Bay, New Guinea. Following one skirmish, Archie was so heroic that the Australians decided to honor him by naming a point of geography after him, "Roosevelt Ridge." Archie was beyond fearless. He told fellow troops not to worry about anything, that he had already been wounded three times and "three's the charm," when a grenade exploded sending shrapnel into his old leg wounds. It was serious enough that the army again declared Archie 100 percent disabled. To this day Archie Roosevelt remains the only man in the history of the American armed services to be classified twice as 100 percent disabled. It was January 1944.[24]

In early 1942, Colonel Theodore Roosevelt, Jr., was promoted to Brigadier General for outstanding leadership. His wife Eleanor was serving too—as nurse once again. And so was Ted's son, Quentin II. Quentin Roosevelt II was a Second Lieutenant serving in Africa. He was wounded by a bullet through the lung from a German Messerschmitt (fighter plane) at Kasserine. He had already been awarded the Silver Star and the Croix de Guerre. He was sent home to convalesce, where he was attended to by his grandmother Edith Roosevelt.[25] But he was not done—he would return to fight again.

The Invasion of Normandy came soon enough (D-Day, June 6, 1944). Ted Jr. would lead the first wave assaulting the beach. He would be the only general in the first amphibious wave at Normandy. And, at 57 years old, he was also the oldest man to hit the beach. Prior to landing the assault he sent this letter to Eleanor:

"We are starting on the great venture of the war, and by the time you get this, for better or for worse, it will be history.

We are attacking by daylight the most heavily fortified coast in history, a shore held by excellent troops. We are throwing excellent troops against it, well armed and backed by good air and naval support.

We are on our transports, buttoned up, our next stop France. The Germans know we are coming, for the harbors of southern England have been crowded with our shipping and the roads choked with our convoys.

The Great Adventure--Untold

I don't think I've written you that I go in with the assault wave and hit the beach at H-Hour. I'm doing it because it's the way I can contribute most. It steadies the young men to know that I am with them, to see me plodding along with my cane. We've got to break the crust with the first wave or we're sunk, for the following groups won't get in. At first Tubby Barton didn't want me to do this, but eventually he agreed after I'd written a formal letter stating my reasons. Quentin goes in, I believe, at H plus 60. That's bad enough. Frankly, it may be worse than when I go in.

We've had a grand life and I hope there'll be more. Should it chance that there's not, at least we can say that in our years together we've packed enough for ten ordinary lives. We've known joy and sorrow, triumph and disaster, all that goes to fill the pattern of human existence. Our children are grown and our grandchildren are here. We have been very happy. I pray we may be together again.

This will be the last for the present. The ship is dark; the men are going to their assembly stations. Before going on deck they sit in darkened corridors to adjust their eyes. Soon the boats will be lowered. Then we'll be off."

General Theodore Roosevelt, Jr., wasn't the only Roosevelt hitting the beach that day. His son Quentin II was also there—Ted at Utah Beach and Quentin II at Omaha Beach. They were the only father-son team participating in the assault. Ted's boat was the first one to hit the beach. He led the assault with a cane in one hand and a 45-caliber pistol in the other. Once the first assault group scaled the sea wall, he went back to lead a second assault group, then another. The men were overwhelmed and inspired to heights of uncommon valor at the sight of this 57 year old General fearless in the face of their enemy. He was awarded the Congressional Medal of Honor.

Years later General Omar Bradley was asked what was the most heroic act he had seen in his 40 years of military service—he described General Roosevelt at Utah Beach.[26]

Five weeks later, Ted Jr. died from a heart attack. He had been promoted to Major General. With his service in both WWI and WWII, he would become the most decorated soldier to serve at the end of World War II. His father would have been proud—his son certainly was. Quentin II stood at attention while volleys were fired and two bugles played taps in echo fashion. The honorary pallbearers Generals Omar Bradley, George Patton, Collins, Huebner, Barton, and Hodges stood at attention. Ted Jr. was buried at Sainte-Laurent-Sur-Mer, near Normandy, the 26th anniversary of the day his brother Quentin died. Following Ted's burial, Quentin's body was removed from Chamery and brought to Normandy to lie next to Ted's.[27] Kermit's body remains in the Aleutians.

This great American saga continues. Four of TR's grandsons joined the CIA. Kermit Roosevelt, Jr., became a legendary figure in the CIA. Quentin II died in the air over China in 1949, and in Roosevelt tradition is buried there, an American hero. Theodore Roosevelt IV did two tours in Viet Nam as a Navy Seal with distinguished honor. There are others—a total of six bear the name Theodore Roosevelt. Americans, ever vigilant were guarding the gates of liberty.

The legacy of Theodore Roosevelt to the American people was not something bequeathed or bought. His legacy resides in his character and that of his family.

"Character, in the long run, is the decisive factor in the life of an individual."
Theodore Roosevelt

"Each man of them knows very well that he could wish no happier lot to his boy in the cradle than that he might grow up to be such a man as Theodore Roosevelt." [28]

John Hay

ENDURING WORDS

The character of a person is ultimately judged by their deeds, and the deeds are often first measured by their words. Words have power—good or bad. The Presidents whose images are carved on Mt. Rushmore left a legacy of both deeds and words that shaped their characters and the character of our nation. If one examines the written or spoken words of a person and reconciles those words to that person's deeds, then their character becomes evident. Adolf Hitler, who needs no introduction, mastered the skills of an orator with words to energize one of the most ingenious and industrious people on earth—the Germans, but only to lead them to destruction with his deeds. The annals of history are heavily burdened with characters that fit this mold. Interestingly, their words are mostly forgotten—but not their deeds.

The greatest words ever spoken or the greatest words ever written have to transcend time and meet the test of exemplary character or they become meaningless words stored upon the trash heap of history. Enduring words are carved in stone, molded in steel, encased in glass or etched on the hearts of uncounted generations.

> *"Ask not what your country can do for you.*
> *Ask what you can do for your country."*
> President John F. Kennedy

When President Kennedy spoke these words he was speaking specifically to the American people. Not the Europeans, not the Communist Nations, and not those of the United Nations. Why, because these words ring hollow unless the citizenry of that country has embraced the twin sisters of "Liberty and Freedom." The message is that you, the American citizen, have the freedom to choose a cause that is greater than yourself, and that cause can be your country and can be what it stands for! Liberty!

"Let every nation know . . . that we shall pay any price, bear any burden, meet any hardship, support any friend, oppose any foe, to assure the survival and the success of liberty."
President John F. Kennedy

Patrick Henry said it another way:

". . . is life so dear, or peace so sweet, as to be purchased at the price of chains and slavery? Forbid it, Almighty God! I know not what course others may take; but as for me, give me liberty or give me death!"

These are enduring and profound words. But it was Thomas Jefferson, the guy on Mt. Rushmore between George Washington and Teddy Roosevelt that laid the ink on parchment that's encased in glass—The Declaration of Independence.

"We hold these truths to be self-evident, that all men are created equal, that they are endowed by their Creator with certain unalienable rights, that among these are Life, Liberty and the pursuit of happiness.—That to secure these rights, Governments are

instituted among Men, deriving their just powers from the consent of the government. —That whenever any Form of Government becomes destructive of these ends, it is the right of the People to alter or to abolish it, and to institute new Government . . . ."

When Thomas Jefferson said "their Creator," he was speaking of God. The "certain unalienable rights," that he speaks of are rights that cannot be taken away from us because they are given to us by God. These are powerful, enduring words from the Declaration of Independence that are uniquely American. They not only shaped our country's future, but also laid the foundation of our Constitution. A Constitution unlike any established in world history before or since and one that defines our national character as a free and brave people who cherish "Liberty for all." Thomas Jefferson concludes the Declaration of Independence with,

"—And for the support of this Declaration, with a firm reliance on the protection of divine Providence [protection provided by God] we mutually pledge to each other our lives, our fortunes, and our sacred honor."

The following statements expressed by Thomas Jefferson differentiate Americans from the rest of the world. The concept that the people have a right to keep and bear arms, not only to protect themselves but also to protect themselves from their own government is uniquely American.

"No free man shall ever be debarred the use of arms."

"The strongest reason for the people to retain the rights to keep and bear arms is, as a last resort, to protect themselves against tyranny in government."

"The tree of liberty must be refreshed from time to time with the blood of patriots and tyrants."

No country, no government, no people are perfect. If we accept that the contemporary American character was forged during the Revolutionary War, then our character was further tempered and gilt-honed in a furnace of hell on earth during our very own Civil War. More Americans died during the Civil War than in all of the wars we have fought combined, to this very day. All to preserve our Union and right the wrongs of our national character!

". . . that from these honored dead we take increased devotion to that cause for which they gave the last full measure of devotion—that we here highly resolve that these dead shall not have died in vain—that this nation, under God, shall have a new birth of freedom—and that government of the people, by the people, for the people, shall not perish from the earth."
Abraham Lincoln, Gettysburg Address

Writers, historians, academics can forever debate and search for the greatest words ever spoken. Some will point to eloquence, brevity, profundity. Do the words stand the test of time? Have they affected the course of history? In all of the words emanating from the American Experience, one cannot overlook those of Abraham Lincoln. Our public schools teach and have popularized the

Gettysburg Address as the defining document produced by Lincoln. Indeed, it is a masterful and eloquent piece, but it is Lincoln's Second Inaugural Address, March 4, 1865, that deserves the highest consideration. This speech that he wrote was short, just two pages, 617 words, and approximately six minutes long. It came at the end of the war, about one month before Robert E. Lee surrendered at Appomattox. The Oath was administered by the Chief Justice. President Lincoln placed his left hand on the Bible which was opened to the fifth chapter of Isaiah. In the crowd in front of the platform were the famous Fredrick Douglass and the infamous John Wilkes Booth. The speech concluded with following:

"With malice toward none, with charity for all, with firmness in the right as God gives us to see the right, let us strive on to finish the work we are in, to bind up the nation's wounds, to care for him who shall have borne the battle and for his widow and his orphan, to do all which may achieve and cherish a just and lasting peace among ourselves and with all nations."

The total speech contains four pieces of Scripture taken from the Bible and includes 13 references to God, The Almighty and the Lord. It is sometimes referred to as the "malice toward none" speech. The words "malice toward none" set the tone for healing a bloodied, war-weary people, and a broken nation. The message of reconciliation and healing was manifested just 35 days later at Appomattox. When Lee surrendered to Grant, there were more tears than cheers. In fact, the Union troops were told not to cheer. The

Confederate Officers were allowed to keep their side arms, and all Confederate soldiers were free to keep the horses they owned and just go home—unimpeded by Federal forces. Five days later, Abraham Lincoln was assassinated.

The healing began on the day of Lincoln's Second Inaugural Address. Lincoln reached back in history to Thomas Jefferson's "Divine Providence" to find the words he needed. The task was so great, his burden so heavy that he relied totally on God's help to give him the words that he could give to the people to bind the wounds on their hearts and heal a hurting nation. So profound was this moment in history, not just for America, but for the world also, that one is given to speculate about what might have happened had America not united behind one flag, and those words. What country, what League of Nations, what world power could have intervened just 50 years later, and for over a period of another 50 years, defeat the evils of Fascism, Nazism, and Communism, liberating hundreds of millions of people? Only one—the United States of America! A country nurtured with great and profound words.

The images of the Presidents on Mt. Rushmore are there because they were men of great character, and their words gave rise to great deeds. Profound words that created the foundation of our country and our Government, words that have endured for more than 235 years that define who we are as a people. Will those words stand the test of time? If America were to cease to exist, would the words survive and be adopted by a succeeding nation and its people? The greatest words ever spoken or written must have to meet that test. But to find these words, we have to go back in history farther than a mere 235 years. Indeed, we will have to reach all the way back into antiquity.

Moses brought mankind words carved in stone that have endured for 3,457 years—The Ten Commandments. These words are the foundation for common law and mores of civilizations to this day: Thou shall not murder, Thou shall not steal, Thou shall not bear false witness against thy neighbor . . . . However, before Moses delivered the Ten Commandments to the Israelites he had been called by God to lead the Israelites out of bondage and into the Promised Land. The Israelites had been slaves of Egyptian Pharaohs for over 400 years and now Moses, at 80 years old, was God's chosen leader to deliver God's people. Moses was not a man without fault. His character, however, is never questioned, even though he had committed murder and became a fugitive of Pharaoh's justice. But worse yet, he would trespass in disobedience against God's will. For the latter offense, he himself would not be allowed to enter the Promised Land. Moses died on Mt. Nebo, overlooking The Promised Land at 120 years old. But, he had delivered God's chosen people! And the chosen words!

Moses delivered the Ten Commandments and spoke the words to the Israelites, but the words were not his. The Ten

Commandments came from God. God spoke the words to Moses and the words are still with us to this day. Consider for a moment words that leave absolutely no doubt about the character of the individual, words that have endured the test of time and even changed the course of history, words that have affected and united hundreds of millions of people. Once again, we are compelled to revisit antiquity, over 2,000 years ago—the words of Jesus of Nazareth.

CHARACTER OF LOVE

In his book *The Greatest Words Ever Spoken*, author Steven K. Scott makes the following succinct and illustrative statement on the life of Jesus.

"No theologian or historian would dispute the fact that Jesus was the single most influential figure ever to walk the earth. His actions, words, and miracles changed the course of history. He inspired entire societies to incorporate compassion and mercy into their cultures. He redefined the standards of morality. He not only changed the course of nations, He brought an unexplainable measure of purpose, peace, and joy into the lives of hundreds of millions of individuals." [29]

One does not have to be a Christian to understand who Jesus of Nazareth is. His words and deeds tell us who he is. His character is built around one word, "Love." He is the only human being widely acknowledged as being "sinless" before God. He challenged existing religion and brought forward the concepts of forgiveness and compassion where none existed before. He performed hundreds upon hundreds of documented miracles, not to his personal enrichment but to the benefit of others. He occupies no grave. World calendars are divided into two times, B.C. (Before Christ) and A.D. (Anno Domini—in the year of our Lord, today's time). His life impacted history 2,000 years ago and still does today.

Jesus said,

"Heaven and earth will pass away, but my words will never pass away." (Matt 24:5)

The following pieces of Scripture provide a glimpse of Jesus—his character and his person.

"But I tell you who hear me: Love your enemies, do good to those who hate you, [28]bless those who curse you, pray for those who mistreat you. [29]If someone strikes you on one cheek, turn to him the other also. If someone takes your cloak, do not stop him from taking your tunic. [30]Give to everyone who asks you, and if anyone takes what belongs to you, do not demand it back. [31]Do to others as you would have them do to you." (Luke 6:27-31)

"But love your enemies, do good to them, and lend to them without expecting to get anything back. Then your reward will be great, and you will be sons of the Most High, because he is kind to the ungrateful and wicked. [36]Be merciful, just as your Father is merciful." (Luke 6:35-36)

"Do not judge and you will not be judged. Do not condemn, and you will not be condemned. Forgive and you will be forgiven. [38]Give and it will be given to you. A good measure, pressed down, shaken together and running over, will be poured into your lap. For with the measure you use, it will be measured to you."
(Luke 6:37-38)

Words such as these had never been spoken by anyone prior to Jesus of Nazareth. They do not require a lot of interpretation or analysis. Simply put, they are words of extraordinary love and forgiveness. Judge not . . . Condemn not . . . and Forgive. Simple words, but simple words that mankind cannot live by!

"But I tell you that men will have to give account on the Day of Judgment for every careless word they have spoken. [37]For by

your words you will be acquitted and by your words you will be condemned." (Matt 12:36-37)

Here, Jesus is referring to the accountability to God for the words we use and their consequences. When Abraham Lincoln said, "A house divided against itself cannot stand," he was referencing the words of Jesus. When Ronald Reagan spoke of, "a shining city on a hill," it was a reference to "a city upon a hill," taken from the Sermon on the Mount given by Jesus, and there are many other examples of words throughout history borrowed from Jesus, and properly so, since he came to deliver a timeless message based on words and deeds.

In brief, Jesus claimed to be the Son of God, and that God sent him to deliver a message to all people. This message was not just for the god-fearing Jewish people, but it was for the Gentiles and non-believers alike. Jesus claimed that through him, he could lead a person into an intimate relationship with God the Father. That sin could be forgiven, and that a person could be made new through the confession of sin and repentance of sin, that is to stop from committing sin and turn to God. That person then would be "born again" and have eternal life through the love of God.

"For God so loved the world that he gave his only begotten Son, that whosoever believes in him shall not perish but have eternal life. For God did not send his son into the world to condemn the world, but to save the world through him." (John 3:16-17)

"I am the way and the truth and the life. No one comes to the Father except through me." (John 14:6)

"I tell you the truth, no one can see the Kingdom of God unless he is born again." (John 3:3-8)

The religious leaders at the time, the Jewish Pharisees and Sadducees, felt threatened by these words of Jesus because in effect their power over the people was being usurped, and their authority was being rendered obsolete. To make matters worse for them, Jesus was performing miracles and in the process persuading people, both Jew and Gentile, with the power of his words and deeds.

The Pharisees witnessed the miracles themselves. The evidence was irrefutable, therefore the Pharisees could not deny the miracles. In fact, the hundreds of miracles that Jesus performed were being witnessed by thousands of people. Consider this: Jesus of Nazareth speaking in an open field, no amphitheater with naturally structured acoustics, no bullhorn, no microphone, no big screen, just a man and an audience of 5,000 people. The ones in the back could not hear him. The ones in the front would relay back what he was saying, but they came anyway. Not just to hear the words but to witness the miracles.

The situation finally became untenable for the Pharisees when witnesses came forward to inform them that Jesus had raised Lazarus from the dead. Lazarus was in a tomb, dead for four days, and was now walking around. This was not the first time that Jesus had raised someone from the dead, it was the third time. But, it was more than the Pharisees could stand and from this time forward they planned the death of Jesus.

Jesus continued to demonstrate the miracles that he could make the blind see, the lame walk, the deaf hear, and raise the dead. He even cured ten lepers of leprosy, all at one time. Jesus didn't make a big production of healing the lepers. He simply said,

"Go, show yourselves to the priests." (Luke 17:11-14)

They were healed! By showing themselves to the priests, they would eventually be allowed to reenter society. It became additional, irrefutable evidence of the power of his words and the authority by which Jesus spoke them.

Indeed, there is no evidence in history of anyone having witnessed the miracles of Jesus ever doubting their authenticity. Even Nicodemus, a highly respected Jewish Pharisee and member of the Jewish ruling council, came to see Jesus one night and said,

"Rabbi, we know that you are a teacher from God, for no one can do these signs that you do unless God is with him."
(John 3:1-2)

Jesus then proceeded to explain to Nicodemus the necessity of being "born again." (John 3:5) In the end, it was Nicodemus himself who helped prepare the body of Jesus for burial.

Jesus said, *"All authority in heaven and on earth has been given to me . . . ."* (Matt 28:20)

Eventually the Pharisees sent officers to arrest Jesus, but they returned empty handed. The Pharisees asked why they hadn't brought him to them. The officers answered, *"No man ever spoke like this man."* (John 7:45)

Indeed, no man had ever spoken the words that Jesus spoke. Not then, not before, and not to this day. Equally important, he backed up his words with his deeds. The miracles confirmed his authority. And that authority with which he spoke the words could only have come from God, because no one before or since has possessed such authority and power.

When Jesus said, *"Destroy this temple and in three days I will raise it up,"* he was not talking about the building he was standing in—he was talking about his body. (John 2:19)

Jesus said concerning his life,

". . . I lay down my life that I may take it again. No one takes it from me, but I lay it down of myself. I have power to lay it down, and I have power to take it again. This command I have received from my Father." (John 10:17-18)

How can a man speak these words, have these words manifest in him as absolute truth, and be just a man? When John the Baptist first saw Jesus coming toward him, he said, *"Behold the*

Lamb of God, who takes away the sin of the world!" John the Baptist declared that Jesus was more than just a man he was also the sacrificial Lamb of God. (John 1:36)

Jesus did not come into the world just to die for man's sins, but he came so that through him man might have eternal life. The message of his words never changed, nor did his character, not even in the face of a brutal death. Not then and not 2,000 years later.

Eventually the Pharisees got their way. They convinced the Roman Governor Pontius Pilate to crucify Jesus. Pilate believed Jesus was innocent of the false charges brought against him. But Pilate acquiesced to the will of the Pharisees and ruling council and had Jesus tortured, scourged, and nailed to a wooden cross.

When asked to defend himself against the charges, Jesus declined. Why? He surely could have found the words! He possessed awesome power and had demonstrated his authority to use it. He willingly went to the cross because it was his mission. He said so many times. He came to die for the sins of man, so that through him man could enter into a personal relationship with God, and have eternal life.

They crucified the only person in history, universally acknowledged to have never broken one of the Ten Commandments, and to have never sinned.

So Jesus of Nazareth came to die and to live! He told his disciples this several times. It was pre-ordained and prophesied hundreds of years prior to his arrival and crucifixion.

More than 755 years before Jesus, the great prophet Isaiah confirmed the prophecy of the coming Messiah (God's anointed one).

"Therefore the Lord Himself will give you a sign; Behold the virgin shall conceive and bear a son, and call his name Immanuel."
(Is 7:14)
"The Spirit of the Lord shall rest upon Him." (Is. 11:2)

"Then the eyes of the blind shall be opened, and the ears of the deaf shall be unstopped. Then the lame shall leap like a deer. And the tongue of the dumb sing." (Is. 35:5-6)

"He was oppressed and he was afflicted, yet He opened not His mouth; He was led as a lamb to the slaughter, and as a sheep before its shears is silent. So He opened not His mouth." (Is. 53:7)

"Because he poured out His soul unto death, and He was numbered with the transgressors and he bore the sin of many, and made intercession for the transgressors." (Is. 53:12)

These are only six of more than 60 prophecies concerning Jesus' fulfillment of the prophecies. But it is the words and the actions of Jesus that carry the overwhelming scrutiny of truth. It matters not whether you are Jew or Gentile, Pharisee or Samaritan, Christian or agnostic, free spirit or no spirit, truth is truth! He spoke certain words. It is a matter of undeniable, irrefutable fact, supported by an overwhelming preponderance of evidence. The character of

Jesus stands on his words backed up by his deeds, and it is precisely his words and deeds which humanity is left with that set him apart from any other man.

Numerous times Jesus foretold of the sacrifice he would make. And he strictly warned and commanded them to tell this to no one, saying,

"The Son of Man must suffer many things, and be rejected by the elders and chief priests and scribes, and be killed, and raised the third day." (Luke 9:21). Then he said to them,

"Thus it is written, and thus it was necessary for the Christ to suffer and to rise from the dead the third day, and that repentance and remission of sins should be preached in His name to all nations, beginning at Jerusalem." (Luke 24:46-47)

"Let these words sink down into your ears for the Son of Man is about to be betrayed into the hands of men." (Luke 9:44)

"Behold, we are going up to Jerusalem, and the Son of Man will be betrayed to the chief priests and to the scribes; and they will condemn Him to death and deliver Him to the Gentiles, and they will mock Him, and scourge Him, and spit on Him, and kill Him. And the third day he will rise again. (Mark 10:33-34)

Jesus knew that they desired to ask Him, and He said to them,

"Are you inquiring among yourselves about what I said, A little while, and you will not see Me; and again a little while, and you will see Me? Most assuredly, I say to you that you will weep and lament, but the world will rejoice; and you will be sorrowful, but your sorrow will be turned into joy. A woman, when she is in labor,

has sorrow because her hour has come; but as soon as she has given birth to the child, she no longer remembers the anguish for the joy that a human being has been born into the world. Therefore you now have sorrow; but I will see you again and your heart will rejoice, and your joy no one will take from you." (John 16:19-22)

"I came forth from the Father and have come into the world. Again, I leave the world and go to the Father." (John 16:28)

And He took the bread, gave thanks and broke it and gave it to them, saying:

"This is My body which is given for you; do this in remembrance of Me." (Luke 22:19)

When Jesus went to the cross, the disciples were not with him. Judas Iscariot, the one who betrayed Jesus (another prediction Jesus had made) had committed suicide. The other 11 had scattered and went into hiding in fear of their own lives. They were shocked and in disbelief that what Jesus had told them had now become real. But why were they in disbelief? They had seen all of the miracles, and heard all of the words, but they could not believe that Jesus, "the Messiah" would willingly subject himself to a torturous death to fulfill the scriptures of the Bible and the words that he had spoken! For them it was just too much to bear. Hanging from the cross, Jesus said among his last words,

"Father forgive them for they do not know what they do."
(Luke 23:34)

He brought a message of forgiveness and love, and now in his dying breath he was pleading for it. Not for himself, but for others, hardly the words of a mere mortal.

The Bible lays out the story of the resurrection of Jesus in great detail. Three days after his death, the Bible tells us that Jesus was walking and talking to those of his choosing. For 40 days he engaged the lives of approximately 500 individuals, beginning with Mary Magdalene, the 11 disciples, and the Apostle Peter among others. The disciples had seen Jesus raise three people from the dead, was it not possible that he could raise himself? In front of everyone present, Jesus asked the disciple Thomas to place his finger on the nail wound of his hands and to touch the wound in his side where he had been speared. It was the very appearance and the words Jesus spoke that restored the faith of Thomas and the other disciples. The resurrection of Jesus and the fulfillment of his words had such an impact on the original apostles that their lives would never be the same again. It is believed that most if not all were killed and died the cruel deaths of martyrs, and mostly by crucifixion.

- Peter was crucified upside down in Rome.
- James, brother of John, was beheaded.
- Andrew, Peter's brother, was crucified.
- Philip was crucified.
- Bartholomew (Nathaniel) skinned alive, was crucified.

- Matthew was axed to death.

- Thomas was speared to death.

- James, son of Alphaeus, was beaten to death with a club after being crucified and stoned.

- Jude was crucified.

- Simon was crucified.

- Matthias, who replaced Judas Iscariot, is believed to have been burned to death.

- The Apostle Paul was beheaded in Rome.

- Only John is believed to have died of natural causes while exiled on the Island of Patmos.

The details of their death are not important, but rather why they died—because they would not deny Jesus Christ—the words he had spoken, the things they had witnessed, or the character of the "Son of Man."

Napoleon Bonaparte—the great military genius, Emperor of France, and conqueror of nations—was no icon of virtue, but he eloquently illuminated the character of Jesus with the following narrative:

(While exiled on the isle of St. Helena, he called Count Montholon to his side and asked him, "Can you tell me who Jesus Christ was?" The Count declined to respond. Napoleon countered):

Charles Hamman

"Well then, I will tell you. Alexander, Caesar, Charlemagne and I myself have founded great empires; but upon what did these creations of our genius depend? Upon force. Jesus alone founded His empire upon love, and to this very day millions will die for Him . . . . I think I understand something of human nature; and I tell you, all these were men, and I am a man: none else is like Him; Jesus Christ was more than man . . . . I have inspired multitudes with such an enthusiastic devotion that they would have died for me . . . but to do this it was necessary that I should be visibly present with the electric influence of my looks, my words, of my voice. When I saw men and spoke to them, I lighted up the flame of self-devotion in their hearts . . . . Christ alone has succeeded in so raising the mind of man toward the unseen, that it becomes insensible to the barriers of time and space. Across a chasm of eighteen hundred years, Jesus Christ makes a demand which is beyond all others to satisfy; he asks for that which a philosopher may seek in vain at the hands of his friends, or a father of his children, or a bride of her spouse, or a man of his brother. He asks for the human heart; He will have it entirely to Himself. He demands it unconditionally; and forthwith His demand is granted. Wonderful! In defiance of time and space, the soul of man, with all its powers and faculties, becomes an annexation to the empire of Christ. All who sincerely believe in Him, experience that remarkable, supernatural love toward Him. This phenomenon is accountable; it is altogether beyond the scope of man's creative powers. Time, the great destroyer, is powerless to extinguish this sacred flame; time can neither exhaust its strength nor put a limit to its range. This is it, which strikes me most; I have often thought of it. This is which proves to me quite convincingly the Divinity of Jesus Christ." [30]

Men of all nations and all persuasions have ascended to greatness through the strength of their character. And men, who are truly great, recognize that their greatness pales when measured against the humility and character of Jesus.

The Great Adventure--Untold

General Douglas McArthur, renowned Commander of the United States Armed Forces, Commander of all United Nation Forces during the Korean War, and Medal of Honor recipient, penned and recited the following prayer at a West Point Graduation Commencement:

> *"Build me a son, O Lord, who will be strong enough to know when he is weak, and brave enough to face himself when he is afraid; one who will be proud and unbending in honest defeat, and humble and gentle in victory.*
>
> *Build me a son whose wishbone will not be where his backbone should be; a son who will know Thee . . . . Lead him, I pray, not in the path of ease and comfort, but under the stress and spur of difficulties and challenge. Here let him learn to stand up in the storm; here let him learn compassion for those who fail.*
>
> *Build me a son whose heart will be clean, whose goal will be high; a son who will master himself before he seeks to master other men; one who will learn to laugh, yet never forget how to weep; one who will reach into the future, yet never forget the past.*
>
> *And after all these things are his, add, I pray, enough of a sense of humor, so that he may always be serious, yet never take himself too seriously. Give him humility, so that he may always remember the simplicity of greatness, the open mind of true wisdom, the meekness of true strength.*
>
> *Then I, his father, will dare to whisper, 'I have not lived in vain.'"*

As we go through life, we affect our character through the choices we make—good, bad, right, or wrong. How we handle the consequences of those choices ultimately will determine whether our character is strengthened positively or negatively. In time of conflict, perhaps we won't always find the right words to offer up with the eloquence of Abraham Lincoln or Thomas Jefferson. Nor will we be able to summon the courage of Marine Lance Corporal Roy Wheat. Nor can we expect to always exhibit the personal leadership of the icon of virtue Theodore Roosevelt. And one thing is certain we will all fall short of demonstrating the faith and love of Jesus of Nazareth. But, we can grow in our faith, and we can always strive to do "the right thing when nobody is looking."

"Greater love has no one than this,
than to lay down one's life for his friends."
(John 15:13—Jesus of Nazareth)

About the Author

Charles Hamman is a Marine combat veteran of the Vietnam War. He served as a Squad Leader and Platoon Guide for the 2nd Battalion 5th Marine Regiment. He is a former Deputy Sheriff with the Horse Mounted Sheriff's Posse where he performed a variety of police duties, including search and rescue. He has been the President of two large subcontracting firms in the construction industry. Currently he resides with his wife Betty on a small horse ranch near Wellington, Colorado.

An avid outdoorsman Charlie likes to spend his recreational time riding horses and mules in the Rocky Mountain West.

Abbreviations

ATS.... *A Time to Stand,* Lord, Walter (Harper & Row, 1961).

CSL.... *Theodore Roosevelt: Champion of the Strenuous Life,* Johnston, William Davidson (Theodore Roosevelt Association, 1958).

LP...... *The Lion's Pride,* Renehan Jr., Edward J. (Oxford University Press, 1998).

M........ *Marine,* Clancy, Tom (The Berkeley Publishing Group, 1996).

PBS.... *Theodore Roosevelt: The Story of Theodore Roosevelt,* (Public Broadcasting Service, 1996).

ROL.... *Recollections of Abraham Lincoln,* Lamon, Ward Hill (Bison Books, 1994).

TBP.... *The Bully Pulpit,* Jeffers, Paul H. (Taylor Publishing Company, 1998).

TLR.... *Theodore Roosevelt: The Last Romantic,* Brands, H. W. (Basic Books, 1997).

TRA.... *Theodore Roosevelt Association Journal.* (Theodore Roosevelt Association).

TWTR...*The Works of Theodore Roosevelt: National Edition,* Roosevelt, Theodore (Charles Scribner & Sons, 1926).

VMHH...*Vietnam Medal of Honor Heroes,* Murphy, Edward (Ballantine Books, 1987).

W........ *Will,* Liddy, G. Gordon (St. Martins Press, 1980, 1996).

Notes

1. Edward Murphy. *Vietnam Medal of Honor Heroes,* (Ballantine Books, 1987), p. 92.

2. H. W. Brands. *Theodore Roosevelt: The Last Romantic,* (Basic Books, 1997), p. 31.

3. H. W. Brands. *Theodore Roosevelt: The Last Romantic,* (Basic Books, 1997), p. 93.

4. Edward J. Renehan, Jr. *The Lion's Pride,* (Oxford University Press, 1998), p. 23.

5. H. W. Brands. *Theodore Roosevelt: The Last Romantic,* (Basic Books, 1997), p. 273.

6. Edward J. Renehan, Jr. *The Lion's Pride,* (Oxford University Press, 1998), p. 31.

7. William Davidson Johnson. *Theodore Roosevelt: Champion of the Strenuous Life,* (Theodore Roosevelt Association, 1958), p. 83.

8. William Davidson Johnson. *Theodore Roosevelt: Champion of the Strenuous Life,* (Theodore Roosevelt Association, 1958), p. 82.

9. Theodore Roosevelt. *The Works of Theodore Roosevelt: National Edition,* (Charles Scribner & Sons, 1926), p. 314, Vol. V.

10. Theodore Roosevelt. *The Works of Theodore Roosevelt: National Edition,* (Charles Scribner & Sons, 1926), 187-224, Vol. XIX.

11. H. W. Brands. *Theodore Roosevelt: The Last Romantic,* (Basic Books, 1997), p. 783.

12. Edward J. Renehan, Jr. *The Lion's Pride,* (Oxford University Press, 1998), p. 133-132.

13. Edward J. Renehan, Jr. *The Lion's Pride,* (Oxford University Press, 1998), p. 191.

14. Edward J. Renehan, Jr. *The Lion's Pride,* (Oxford University Press, 1998), p. 151-152.

15. Edward J. Renehan, Jr. *The Lion's Pride,* (Oxford University Press, 1998), p. 194.

16. Edward J. Renehan, Jr. *The Lion's Pride,* (Oxford University Press, 1998), p. 196.

17. Edward J. Renehan, Jr. *The Lion's Pride,* (Oxford University Press, 1998), p. 197-206.

18. Edward J. Renehan, Jr. *The Lion's Pride,* (Oxford University Press, 1998), p. 207.

19. Edward J. Renehan, Jr. *The Lion's Pride,* (Oxford University Press, 1998), p. 228.

20. Edward J. Renehan, Jr. *The Lion's Pride,* (Oxford University Press, 1998), p. 229.

21. Edward J. Renehan, Jr. *The Lion's Pride,* (Oxford University Press, 1998), p. 232.

22. Edward J. Renehan, Jr. *The Lion's Pride,* (Oxford University Press, 1998), p. 232.

23. Edward J. Renehan, Jr. *The Lion's Pride,* (Oxford University Press, 1998), p. 232.

24. Edward J. Renehan, Jr. *The Lion's Pride,* (Oxford University Press, 1998), p. 233.

25. Edward J. Renehan, Jr. *The Lion's Pride,* (Oxford University Press, 1998), p. 234.

26. Edward J. Renehan, Jr. *The Lion's Pride,* (Oxford University Press, 1998), p. 237.

27. Edward J. Renehan, Jr. *The Lion's Pride,* (Oxford University Press, 1998), p. 239.

28. James G. Barber. *Theodore Roosevelt Icon of the American Century,* (Smithsonian Institute, 1998), p. 8.

29. Steven K. Scott . *The Greatest Words Ever Spoken,* (Waterbrook Press, 2008).

30. Henry Parry Liddon. *Liddon's Bampton Lectures,* (Rivingtons, 1869), p. 148.

Bibliography

Barber, James G. *Theodore Roosevelt Icon of the American Century.* Smithsonian Institution, 1998.

Brands, H. W. *Theodore Roosevelt: The Last Romantic. Basic Books,* 1997.

Clancy, Tom. *Marine.* Berkeley Publishing Group, 1996.

Cohen, Stan. *Images of the Spanish-American War.* Pictorial Histories Publishing Co., 1997.

Davis, Kenneth C. *Don't Know Much About History,* Avon Books, 1993.

Encyclopedia International. Grolier, 1972.

Gores, Stan. *The Attempted Assassination of Teddy Roosevelt (Wisconsin Stories).* State Historical Society of Wisconsin, 1980.

Jeffers, H. Paul. *The Bully Pulpit.* Taylor Publishing Co., 1998.

Johnston, William Davidson. *Theodore Roosevelt: Champion of the Strenuous Life.* The Theodore Roosevelt Association, 1958.

Lamon, Ward Hill. *Recollections of Abraham Lincoln.* Bison Books, 1994.

Liddon, Henry Parry. *Liddon's Bampton Lectures.* Rivington, 1869.

Liddy, G. Gordon. *Will.* St. Martins Press, 1996.

Lord, Walter. *A Time to Stand.* Harper & Row, 1961.

Marquis, Thomas B. *Keep the Last Bullet for Yourself.* Reference Publications, Inc., 1976.

Moskin, J. Robert. *The U.S. Marine Corps Story.* McGraw Hill, 1992.

Murphy, Edward. *Vietnam Medal of Honor Heroes.* Ballantine Books, 1987.

Murphy, Jack. *History of the U.S. Marines.* Bison Books, 1984.

New King James Version. Thomas Nelson, Inc., 1982.

Scott, Steven K . *The Greatest Words Ever Spoken.* Waterbrook Press, 2008.

Books by Pearn and Associates, Inc.

The Great Adventure—Untold, Charles Hamman, nonfiction, cloth*
Cowboy Up, Ryan Thorburn, nonfiction, paper
1945, Joseph J. Kozma, novel, paper*
Light Across the Alley, The Story of a Young Matchmaker,
    Victor W. Pearn (Fiction) Kindle Books only*
Dream Season, My Brother Gary and the 1957 Ashland Panthers
    Victor W. Pearn (Biography) Kindle Books only*
Until We Meet, Joseph J. Kozma (Poetry) paperback
It Started & Ended: **The Story About a Soldier and Civilian**
    Life, Bud Grounds (Biography) paper
Lost Cowboys: The Bud Daniel Story, and Wyoming Baseball,
    Ryan Thorburn (Biography) paper
Black 14: The Rise, Fall and Rebirth of Wyoming Football,
    Ryan Thorburn (Biography) paper
The Dreamer and the Dream, Rick E. Roberts (Poetry) paper
Mathematics in Color, Joseph J. Kozma (Poetry) paper
Walking in Snow, John Knoepfle (Poetry) paper
I Look Around for my Life, John Knoepfle (Biography) cloth
    and Kindle*
A Lenten Journey Toward Christian Maturity, William E. Breslin
    (Prayer Guide) paper
Ikaria: A Love Odyssey on a Greek Island, Anita Sullivan
    (Biography) paper and Kindle*
The U Book, Photo Travel Journal in India, Nathan Pierce
    (Poetry & Biography — publisher only) full color paper
Another Chance, Joe Naiman, (Fiction — publisher only) cloth
Goulash and Picking Pickles, Louise Hoffmann (Biography) cloth
Point Guard, Victor Pearn (Fiction) cloth

Available on Barnesandnoble.com, Amazon.com, (also available from
Ingram Books and Baker and Taylor) you may order from your local
bookstore, or from the publisher — Pearn and Associates, Inc.
happypoet@hotmail.com/970-599-8924.
*Available on Kindle Books.

CPSIA information can be obtained at www.ICGtesting.com
Printed in the USA
237774LV00002B/1/P